Sigh
See
Start

Sigh
See

A Science-Based
Method in
Three Simple Steps

Start

HOW TO BE THE PARENT
YOUR CHILD NEEDS
IN A WORLD THAT WON'T
STOP PUSHING

Alison Escalante, MD

PA PRESS

PRINCETON ARCHITECTURAL PRESS · NEW YORK

PUBLISHED BY
Princeton Architectural Press
A division of Chronicle Books LLC
70 West 36th Street
New York, NY 10018
papress.com

27 26 25 24   4 3 2 1   First edition

ISBN 978-1-7972-2366-7

EDITOR: Jennifer Thompson
DESIGNER: Paul Wagner

Library of Congress Control Number: 2023942965

To Miles and Connor

CONTENTS

Preface

I have always been keenly aware of what an honor it is to be trusted with the care of people's children. After all, I became a pediatrician because I was so passionate about the welfare of children. I wanted to care for them when they were sick or suffering, and help them have everything they needed to grow up happy, healthy, and thriving. My favorite part of the job is the opportunity to coach parents on how to support their children's development. While I did receive excellent training in pediatrics, the one thing my training did not prepare me for was the growing level of anxiety and perfectionism in parents. As a parent to young children, I recognized myself every day in the parents I saw distracted by anxiety and disconnected from the kids right in front of them. They didn't realize that their example was teaching their kids to worry, too, and that's not healthy for anyone.

Determined to break through this, I read every parenting book I could find. None of them seemed to have an answer, and many of them pushed the same anxious perfectionism I was already seeing in parents. These books told me that I was going to mess up my kids for life if I made the littlest mistakes, but they vehemently disagreed with each other about what counted as mistakes. I was struck by how different these attitudes were from the ones I saw in my own parents' generation. They worried, of course, but they were also confident in their parenting abilities.

That's when I thought back to what I had learned pursuing my undergraduate degree in the history of culture and ideas, and I realized what was going on. This was not about how individual parents were raising their kids; this was a problem with the entire culture of parenting: a ShouldStorm of conflicting, high-pressure advice. Unless we could see how and why parenting anxiety was being imposed on us, we were never going to get free of that anxiety.

This book was born from my desire to free myself and the parents I served from all the worry that was getting in the way of enjoying our kids. I knew that helping parents see why the advice they were getting was a problem was not going to solve anything; we needed to replace those ideas with better ones. It was years before the solution came to me, but when it did, Sigh, See, Start helped me and the parents I told about it transform our relationships with our kids while meeting their genuine needs. At first, my scientific training made me skeptical. Did my method really work? Would it keep working? But after years of watching what it does in families, there is no denying that when parents use Sigh, See, Start, their own confidence grows quickly. When kids learn that they can trust their parents to meet them where they are, the impact on their development is remarkable.

All too often, parenting books seem to be written for parents with plenty of time, energy, physical and mental health, money, family support, neurotypical kids, and happy heterosexual marriages. As a pediatrician, I know that life rarely works that way, and that any advice I offer families is only valuable if it works in the lives we actually live. Sigh, See, Start does that. As we use Sigh, See, Start, we meet ourselves and our kids where we are right now, with the resources we have (or don't have) right now, and we find connections with our kids and solutions that work for us.

This book is meant to include everyone, which is why it's important to point out that the word *see* is meant metaphorically. The see step in Sigh, See, Start is not meant to exclude parents with visual impairments—it simply means to observe mindfully with whatever tools we have.

The stories I share in this book are stories I've heard not from one family, but from dozens. They were drawn from a variety of sources, and in many cases details from different accounts have been combined and names have been changed to respect privacy. Those that came from interviews have been edited for clarity.

I can't wait to share this parenting journey with you!

A Perfect ShouldStorm for Parents

As a parent, there don't seem to be any "right" answers. I'm constantly wondering if I'm making the right decisions for my kids, and I'm struggling.

—Jennie, mother of three

When new parents come into my office, they are often filled with questions: Should we breastfeed? Should we co-sleep with the baby? Should we *not* sleep with the baby? Should we buy a certain toy to encourage development? Should we *not* use that toy? As the children get older, the questions change, but the shoulds stay. Should we allow screen time? Should we have the birds and the bees talk now? Should we do this? Should we *not* do that? There are lots of parents shoulding all over themselves out there, doubting themselves, desperate to get parenting "right."

I call this parenting pursuit of perfection a ShouldStorm. We are continually being messaged by the larger culture that we must try to maximize our opportunities to be the best parents possible at all costs—to worry about, well, everything, and to get it right all the time. Otherwise, the consequences will be dire. We are fully responsible for whatever happens to our children, and the worst thing that our kids can experience is emotional discomfort, because we equate that with trauma, and trauma means permanent damage and evidence of how we've failed our kids. We must keep our kids safe all the time, physically and emotionally. I've had so many loving and engaged parents share with me their fear that they will somehow "mess their child up for life." As a mom, I have had some of the same worry—that I will somehow fail to give my kids the right support or opportunities, and this failure on my part will cause them future suffering.

It's a real ShouldStorm, and it is robbing us of a lot of joy.

We spend more time with our kids than the members of any prior generation, yet there is collective guilt around not spending enough time with our kids—or enough quality time. We do more for our kids than any prior generation, but remain convinced that we are not doing enough. Our parental anxiety is but one part of a larger culture of anxiety, which tells us we should optimize everything to achieve top productivity at work while somehow reaching a maximum level of health and happiness. If we end up unhappy, unhealthy, or burnt out it's probably because we didn't optimize ourselves enough. This is a collective culture that dominates our attention and energy and cuts us off from enjoying our lives. A pre-pandemic Gallup world survey shows that adults in the United States are the most anxious in the world. HealthyWomen, a nonprofit organization dedicated to equipping women with the evidence they need to make health decisions, ran a survey that revealed 96 percent of American women say they have suffered from anxiety, and 81 percent say they suffer from it at least weekly, again before the COVID-19 pandemic sent anxiety rates through the roof. But when our high-pressure culture gets started on parents it becomes the most toxic, because kids are not projects to be optimized. They are human beings to be cherished.

THE SHOULDSTORM DEFINED

The ShouldStorm is a high-pressure culture of criticism and anxiety that pushes perfectionistic parenting. Culture refers to a set of beliefs and behaviors that a group of people take for granted. It influences our friends, family, and neighbors, our online groups, and a huge body of parenting blogs, articles, and books. The ShouldStorm has an opinion on every little thing parents do, but it often contradicts itself. It tells parents what they should or should not do, and threatens that kids will suffer if parents don't follow those shoulds to the letter. Then parents internalize the shoulds; the ShouldStorm lives in our heads and makes parents feel anxiety and shame. Parents end up approaching their kids from a position of frantic worry about getting it right, instead of from their true selves.

There are two important components to understanding our cultural ShouldStorm and its power to make parents feel insecure, anxious, and ashamed: the internal triggers and the external ones. An internal trigger works like this: Your child is being difficult, and you feel anxious because the critical voice in your head is telling you that you should be calm, even as the baby screams in your ear and tears at your hair. The voice says, "You shouldn't let the baby cry like that," but you simply don't know what to do. Perhaps you should follow those three easy steps that you read about in a blog post the other day. You then act on the should, which may not be suited to you and your child in that situation. Your confidence plummets, and you then follow another, different should from someone else. Rather than drawing on your own instincts or experience, you become caught in the vicious cycle of the ShouldStorm. Beware, it always has plenty more shoulds to offer.

The external piece is the messaging that comes from the larger culture, often media or another parent who consumes this same fear-based parenting culture. When a parent is unsure about what to do, they usually look for advice—reasonable enough. But the messages they get are bewildering, often conflicting, and sometimes terrifying. Alana, the mother of a former patient, was in month two of her maternity leave with her first baby. She had yet to figure out how to take a shower while caring for her small baby. She felt like a safe, short period of possible crying might be okay for her child, but she Googled it first. She found articles telling her that her baby would not bond properly if she let her cry. This is not proven by any research, and Alana's instinct disagreed, but it unnerved her. So, she went to her Facebook moms group. The comments poured in, and Alana felt like a terrible mother for considering letting her baby potentially cry for a few minutes. *What did you fail to do in the first place that your baby couldn't be happy for a few minutes? How could you even think of neglecting your child?*

When five minutes of possible fussing is renamed "neglect," know that the ShouldStorm's all-or-nothing toxic thinking is at work. We need and want to parent in community, and parents naturally look for a few go-to resources from whom they can seek advice and support. When the process works well, parents use that advice in concert with their own understanding of their needs and those of their particular child. But this all goes wrong when the ShouldStorm gets into the mix. Whether it masquerades as community or an expert source of advice, the shoulds are shaming, misinformed, and conflicting enough to shut down parents' confidence. As Jessica Winter writes in the *New Yorker*, "The business of parenting advice, though, is to raise the stakes—to say it's all your fault, but that means you're in control and you can fix it."[1] Even worse, the ShouldStorm mixes just enough right-sounding information with all of the misguided shoulds that it leads parents to doubt what they instinctively know about their own children. In reality, there is usually a range of right, and it is different based on families' temperaments, kids, and situations. These are all things that parents need freedom to explore with their children, but they are robbed of that freedom when they are scared into thinking there is but one right way that they just don't yet know.

Nothing Is Ever Enough

Sociologist Caitlyn Collins spent five years studying parenthood in four wealthy Western countries for her 2019 book, *Making Motherhood Work: How Women Manage Careers and Caregiving*, and found that there is a common cultural ideal of motherhood. Sociologists refer to the cluster of beliefs that form an idea like this as a "cultural schemata." In the schemata of mother devotion, a good mother possesses an all-absorbing devotion to her children as the source of her life's meaning, creativity, and fulfillment.

Whether a parent consciously or unconsciously ascribes to wanting to be the perfect mother, these ideas influence parents and their parenting. A recent study by Patrick Ishizuka in Oxford Academic's *Social Forces* found that "cultural norms of child-centered, time-intensive mothering and fathering are now pervasive, pointing to high contemporary standards for parental investments in children."[2] In fact, most experts refer to all the different versions of the way we parent today as "intensive parenting."

While parents, and particularly the primary caregiver, or the *intensive parent*, as I call them, internalize the unrealistic expectations of the ShouldStorm regarding how they should be at home, parents who work outside of the home can get stuck on impossible ideals of home and work. As Collins writes in her book, "Across the countries where I conducted interviews, one desire remained constant among mothers. Women wanted to feel that they were able to combine paid employment and child-rearing in a way that seemed equitable and didn't disadvantage them at home or at work."[3] That means in the United States, where 70 percent of mothers work and have kids under the age of eighteen, drowning in stress is the norm for moms and all parents.

The partners of intensive parents are doing far more than fathers did one generation ago, but the split in what was once known as "women's work," that is childcare and domestic chores, is still far from equal. Jennifer Senior writes about this inequality in her book *All Joy and No Fun: The Paradox of Modern Parenting*, pointing out that in couples with children under the age of six, mothers work five more hours per week than fathers. Much of this shows up at night, when "in dual-earner couples, women were three times more likely than men to report interrupted sleep if they had a child at home under the age of one, and stay-at-home mothers were six times as likely to get up with their children as stay-at-home dads."[4]

Parents are working overtime at home and at work, and they are doing it with significantly less support than previous generations or other parents around the world. Compared to Sweden and other industrialized nations, Collins notes, "The United States is an outlier among Western industrialized countries for its lack of support for working mothers."[5] Indeed, American mothers stood out in Collins's research due to their experience of crushing guilt and work-family conflict. It's so extreme that more women are opting not to have children. In the *Washington Post*, writer Monica Hesse explains her own decision. Hesse's salary range was $37,000 to $45,000 a year during her prime childbearing years, which she noted was far above the minimum wage in the United States. Yet, in the area where she lived, daycare cost an average of $24,000 per year, while the rent on a two-bedroom apartment could cost more than $30,000. Meanwhile, her own mother was still working full-time, meaning she did not have access to free childcare from a family member. "The math never made sense. I did not have children because while other countries determined that investing in child care—making it free or inexpensive—is the easiest way to encourage motherhood, the United States has determined that what's easiest is simply berating families who can't make it work."[6]

Hesse hits on another key component of the ShouldStorm here: berating and publicly shaming families. I've heard endless stories from parents about being shamed by their relatives, their children's daycare providers, in a social media group, or just randomly at Target for not conforming to some ShouldStorm cultural standard of blemish-free perfection. When did it become okay for everyone to comment on another's individual parenting choices?

"What is wrong with your daughter?" an older woman on the street casually asked Nina, a new mom. "Is she sick? What are those marks on her face?"

Nina smiled and told her that it was entirely normal baby acne. But when the woman shook her head in disbelief, it was hurtful. In the Facebook parenting group that I facilitate, Should-Free Parenting, I polled parents about their experiences with public shaming. A full 338 parents responded, and the results were overwhelming: 86 percent said they had been shamed by other mothers, and 50 percent said they had been shamed by everyone!

There were plenty of the expected subjects, like being shamed for bringing too light a jacket for the weather or using formula to feed a baby. But most surprising was how often these mothers were shamed for doing what is recommended by the scientific, medical community, not for doing anything radical or controversial. Moms were shamed for breastfeeding or for keeping their infants in rear-facing car seats.

When Monique talks about her kids, she often mentions her "big plans" for them. Her parents had big plans for her, too, that centered on her finding financial security. But Monique's plans for her daughter are broader. "My mother was extremely close to her mother," Monique told me. "And I'm extremely close to my mother. So, the three of us are always passing things down: every 'mistake' my grandmother made, my mother made, and I made. She [her daughter, Zo] was going to be the one who was not going to make it. So, Zo was going to be so perfect in every single way." This is the impossible goal that drives the ShouldStorm: that we can raise perfect kids who are better than we are in every way.

And until recently, Monique's attempts at parenting perfection were going well. She breastfed Zo until she was four years old; and then when she didn't have milk for her son, she bought breastmilk for him on the internet. Her kids attend a desirable private school, participate in a full range of activities, go to playdates she carefully curates for them, and have their mother's presence whenever they are not elsewhere.

But there was one thing Monique wishes someone had told her before she became a mother: "I wish I had known and understood that your children are their own entity. They're just a whole other human being outside of you." Her daughter, now thirteen years old, has begun disrupting the big plans Monique had for her. "I'm figuring out that's not her plan. She has her own plan. So, I have to sit back as a spectator and just guide her when she wants to be guided." Monique says she's not alone: many of her friends are dealing with the same surprise with their own kids.

The compulsive drive to overdo it can come from a different place for each of us. Early in her marriage, Jane had practiced in a top law firm, but after she had kids, she stayed home with them. She is exhausted from managing her kids' activities, including the tutors to make sure they place well in school. "Sometimes I wish we could cut down, but then I feel I have to justify the fact that I don't work," she told me. The ShouldStorm claims that its pressured brand of parenting is all about the kids, but neither of these well-meaning mothers knew what their kids thought of all this. They were blinded by fears and anxieties.

In single-parent families, our culture creates a crushing weight of stress. Laura strives to make up for the fact that she's the only parent because her kids' father left the family five years ago due to his substance abuse. Laura combines working as the breadwinner with covering both kids' activities and their emotional needs. In short, living up to the ShouldStorm is unworkable for Laura. Recently, her daughter, Emma, developed depression and thoughts of hurting herself. Laura works tirelessly to take Emma to and communicate with Emma's doctors and therapists. "I worry about her risk of suicide and self-harm constantly," said Laura. That fear, along with the nagging voice that constantly asks Laura if she's doing enough for her kids, keeps Laura constantly stuck in the ShouldStorm.

Nothing Is Enough for Dads, Either—But It's Different

It doesn't matter what the gender of one or both parents may be; all parents are subjected to the unrealistic expectations and shaming of the ShouldStorm. However, men are influenced by the ideal of motherhood in ways distinct from the influence on their female parent counterparts. This may, of course, play out differently in different families.

In almost every family I have seen over the last two decades, one of the parents in a two-parent family takes on the intensive parenting role, while the other assumes the dismissed one. I first recognized these roles while caring for the children of same-sex couples, who helped me see beyond gender stereotypes. Indeed, my clinical experience with heterosexual couples has taught me that gender has little to do with who assumes each role.

For example, Jordan is a stay-at-home dad, and he, not his wife, is the intensive parent. Before he was a father, he spent many years as a coach for children's sports, while Jordan's wife had very little experience with children. Yet he confessed to me that he feels belittled or ignored most of the time. "She's a great mom, and I love her, but it's hard," he told me. "I'm the one with the kids all day. But if my wife or any other mother disagrees with me, then I'm wrong. If my kid bumps his head on a cabinet, it's a big deal. It means I wasn't watching him properly. But if he does it when he's with his mom, then it's because he's a kid."

Jordan's story shows the cultural ideal of motherhood at work. The belief that men lack the necessary skills to raise children undermines them when they step up to do it. Even though Jordan is the one at home with the kids and the one who observes them all day, his experience has been that the opinion of any woman who is a mother matters more than his when it comes to his kids. That's something our culture does to parents in a million different ways. It says that the parent who knows their child doesn't know what they are talking about and someone else does.

On the other hand, dads routinely tell me that they don't feel the ShouldStorm's blaming or shaming the way moms do. "Dads get a pass. That's been my perception for sure since I was a kid," Eitan told me. "So, when it's two dads, it's like, oh, you're heroic." His husband, Andrew, echoed the sentiment: "As a two-dad household, anything that we do is kind of miraculous because the expectations for dads are so low."

But that doesn't mean they aren't influenced by the ShouldStorm in other ways. Andrew, an architect and a business owner in New York City, feels the parenting subculture of their neighborhood. He describes living in Park Slope, an affluent neighborhood in Brooklyn, as a cliché of intensive parenting. "It's routine for parents to ask, 'What are your kids doing?' When they were infants, it was, 'Oh, are you teaching your kids sign language?' As they got older it became, 'What afterschool activities are you doing?'" Andrew recalled. "It's hard not to judge yourself when you're like, 'Oh, he's doing Russian math? Oh, she's also doing Russian math?' Is everybody doing Russian math? Should we be doing Russian math?" In Andrew's experience, parents ask these questions for the same reason he does, "I think a lot of it is genuine curiosity. I do think about how many activities our kids do and whether they are being properly stimulated." He also worries they may be overscheduled. His husband shares both these concerns.

As they do for every parent who wonders if their child is overscheduled, all of the activities feel important to Andrew and Eitan. Besides swimming, their kids' activities reflect an appreciation for family and culture. Both Andrew and Eitan were born in the United States and grew up in California, and both had parents who immigrated to the United States from China and Israel, respectively. Their children are adopted: their son is of mixed Chinese and Black ancestry, while their daughter is Afro-Latina. The kids take Chinese and attend what Eitan calls "the most hippy-dippy Hebrew school in New York City." They also take a class in capoeira, an Afro-Brazilian tradition of music, dance, and self-defense that Andrew says is attended almost entirely by Black children. His daughter, who attends a predominantly white public school, has been struggling with her racial identity, and Andrew hopes attending the capoeira class and sharing more time with folks who may look more like she does will help her take pride in something Afro-Brazilian.

Parent guilt is a routine part of our high-pressure culture, something both Andrew and Eitan feel. "I'm always thinking about what I'm doing wrong, and what I could be doing better," said Andrew. "I parent a little bit out of guilt." Meanwhile, Eitan, a Chinese medicine practitioner and business owner, reported the sort of self-blame one often hears from working mothers—feeling guilty for not staying home with the kids for their first year, for not being home enough, for the times he is too tired to play, and even "guilt that I'm not grateful all the time for the experience of being a parent." Even though the kids have had the same "wonderful" and loving nanny for eight years, Eitan immediately blames the fact that he works when something goes wrong with the kids. If only he had stayed home, his son might not have become a picky eater, their behavior might be more perfect, and his daughter might have started speech therapy earlier if he had been there paying attention. (He was. Eitan brought up concerns about her speech at multiple visits where the doctor advised waiting.) And in one of the most classic statements of ShouldStorm-induced parent guilt I've ever heard, Eitan said that if he stayed home with the kids, "I would have the energy to find the best occupational therapist and shuttle her there three times a week, instead of relying on the most convenient occupational therapist because they're willing to come to our house or they're a block away." Eitan has taken on most of the roles of the intensive parent: he's the one who keeps the kids' complex schedules straight and packs their lunches.

Assumptions about dads are still very prominent in Andrew's working world. "Colleagues who may not think about the fact that we're gay parents assume that there must be a wife at home to pick up the kids," he said. "When I say I have to do this or do that [for the kids] they pause like 'Oh, you don't have somebody in your life to take care of that? Can't the nanny do that?'" Andrew wants to be with his kids and finds the assumption that he would prefer to be at work confusing.

Al has also felt the difference in expectations for dads. In his case, his own father and his father-in-law are often surprised if he mentions doing the dishes or changing a diaper. "I was a hero. They couldn't believe I did so much," he told me. Al, who runs operations for a natural gas company, and his wife, a nurse, are raising two daughters. As a dad, Al says he feels little pressure from the Should-Storm, but he doesn't realize how much his approach is influenced by norms of intensive parenting.

For instance, Al observes what he calls "parenting hours" between 7:30 a.m. and 7:30 p.m. while the girls are awake. "That time is theirs, and I'm going to be completely present in that time," said Al. That means whenever he is not at work on weekdays and "90 percent of the time on weekends," Al either directly interacts with his daughters or stays in a room nearby and makes sure not to engage in any activity that will distract him from giving his full attention if the girls walk in to say something. Which they do every ten minutes on average. When Al decided to build a dollhouse for the girls as a Christmas present, parenting hours meant that he would start construction after the girls were in bed and often go until 3:00 a.m. as often as five days a week rather than using their weekend parenting hours. By the time he was done, "It turned into two dollhouses with a shared yard. The whole thing is eight feet wide by five feet tall. It takes up what used to be our dining room…. It's outrageous," Al said. The impossible standards of the ShouldStorm, the parent-shaming that keeps us stuck in it, and the way that it polarizes our parenting relationships, all add up to one thing: parents are burning out.

Parental Burnout

Intensive parenting and the chronic stress of the ShouldStorm are every bit as demanding as a high-pressure career. And that means that parents are now suffering the type of burnout that we used to associate with doctors or social workers. Burnout happens when people work extremely hard without enough support. People who are burned out feel emotionally exhausted, ineffective, and like their work lacks meaning. They also experience symptoms like rigid thinking, irritability, difficulty sleeping, and trouble with attention and memory. Burnout makes people think about quitting their jobs—but, of course, parents can't quit being parents.

Burnout feels terrible. "It's not that I'm stressed out," says one mom in an article by psychologist Robyn Koslowitz in *Psychology Today*. "It's like I've progressed beyond stressed to numb. Managing my kids and their endless needs seems impossible. I'm always messing up."[7] A recent paper published in *Clinical Psychological Science* examined two related studies designed to find out whether parental burnout is different from job burnout. The study found that parental burnout is defined by exhaustion, detachment, and/or a sense of inefficacy, and is a distinct entity from job burnout or clinical depression.[8]

"Burned out parents are exhausted by the unceasing demands of parenting. Although they might have rest periods, they never fully recharge. They're always in survival mode, which of course leads to more exhaustion and stress," writes Koslowitz in her article on the study.

Almost every intensive parent I ask tells me they have experienced parental burnout, and most of them say they feel it currently. Years of pandemic parenting have intensified these feelings substantially for many. "I've definitely experienced parent burnout. All the time, all day," said Monique. And some fathers feel it too. "I feel like I'm in a perpetual state of parental burnout at this point," said Eitan. "I don't experience as much joy in parenting as I used to."

Exhausted parents may have trouble sleeping because burnout is a nasty combination of overstimulation and fatigue. Stress drives the brain to think constantly, and while parents may be physically exhausted, their brains and nervous systems are overstimulated, causing sleep troubles. It can become a vicious cycle, whereby greater stress and fatigue cause greater trouble with sleep. In other cases, detached parents feel like they are going through the motions. They are doing what they need to do for their kids, but they don't take pleasure in their kids or the activities. They find it difficult to express love or warmth to their children, which means the kids are not feeling their love. This makes parents feel terrible about themselves.

And, lastly, many parents feel ineffective. This particularly happens to parents with children who have special needs or intense personalities, because the parents' attempts to help their children don't seem to work. The unrealistic culture tells them they should be able to nurture or manage their children into near-perfection, or at least to be more like "normal" kids; parents feel discouraged when their children's behaviors and struggles persist. Across the board, parenting feels like an overwhelming and impossible task.

A lot of what contemporary parents take for granted as the level of involvement, protection, and comfort a child needs stems from the misuse of attachment theory (which we will get into in Chapter 1). Whether parents know where it came from or not, the idea that babies had to have just the right attachment to their parents in the early years influenced just about everyone. If a parent didn't get the early attachment just right, the theory said, it could never be repaired, and the child was doomed to a bad life. But in reality, the research on attachment shows that perfection is not how you create a secure attachment—not even close. In order for a child to have a secure attachment, the parent needs to be in sync with their child at least 30 percent of the time.[9] We'll go into this in more depth later, but it means that engaged, loving, and well-intentioned parents who are striving to meet the needs of their kids but missed a child's cue two out of three times did not harm the security of their attachment. The kids thrived. Furthermore, research shows those daily and inevitable moments of misattunement, referred to by attachment researchers as "rupture and repair," are necessary to create a secure attachment. When well-loved and cared-for children have to practice self-soothing and self-trust during conflict or frustration with the caregiver, it is a time for them to learn and then experience the strengthening of the bond when repair work is done. It is an integral part of knowing they can endure some stress and that their bond is secure.

As beloved Fred Rogers put it,

> Just as it takes time for children to understand what real love is, it takes time for parents to understand that being always patient, quiet, even-tempered, and respectful isn't necessarily what "good" parents are.... Parents help children by expressing a wide range of feelings—including appropriate anger. All children need to see that the adults in their lives can feel anger and not hurt themselves or anyone else when they feel that way.[10]

* * *

When I explain the fallacies of the ShouldStorm to parents, I watch their eyebrows lift and their shoulders relax. Sometimes they cry with relief. Relief from the constant feeling of failure (or fear of failure) helps parents start to make room for a more compassionate and effective way of being with themselves and their children. But if people are parenting with unrealistic expectations of perfection one hundred percent of the time, the results are parents, as I often see in my office, too anxious or too worried to parent at their best.

It does not have to be this way. The Sigh, See, Start method gives us a way to step out of the anxiety and honestly connect with ourselves and our kids so we can choose our actions more wisely both in the moment and ahead of time. Here's how it works: whenever you feel a should, sigh. Breathe in deeply and let it go long and slow. Sighing helps you calm down and connect with yourself. Next, see. See your child, see their body language, see the situation. Just mindfully observe for a moment without trying to change anything. Then (and only then) start. Start thinking about what makes sense here and then try doing that. You might start something, or you might start nothing to give your child space to work things out for themselves. What you start might work, or it might not, but either way you learn more about your child. And if a mistake triggers guilt, "Oh, I should have done it that way," you know what to do: sigh, see, and start again. With Sigh, See, Start, instead of reacting automatically to the shoulds in your head, you create a continuous loop of learning and growth for you and your child.

How to Use This Book

In Part 1, we'll look at how, over the course of two generations, our culture shifted from a more relaxed parenting approach to the intensive parenting we see today, and we'll hear from kids on how the ShouldStorm impacts them. Then, in Part 2, we'll learn more about the Sigh, See, Start method, why it works, and how to use it to transform the way we parent our kids. For parents who feel it is urgent to get started, it is fine to jump right to Part 2, but I encourage you to come back to the earlier chapters when you can because it's easier to plot a wise course forward if we understand where we started. Finally, in Part 3, we will look at what it means to live with a Sigh, See, Start mindset, and how to meet our kids' genuine needs proactively by using some of the best science-based techniques that complement Sigh, See, Start.

PART 1

LIFE IN THE SHOULDSTORM

Chapter 1

How Did We End Up in a ShouldStorm?

At least once a day, I feel like the worst mom in the world, and I cry in my car.

—Amy in the movie *Bad Moms*

My undergraduate work at Princeton University was on the way ideas can change cultures. This can happen for a lot of reasons: events, wars, economics, pandemics, and all sorts of other factors come into play. But nothing seems to bring change faster than when a powerful idea takes hold. Sometimes within a generation, an entire society can make an about-face and go the opposite direction of the one before under the influence of powerful ideas. And that's exactly what has happened to parents. Standards for what kids were allowed to do were different just one generation ago. One of my older colleagues used to run errands for his mother, going alone to the store when he was in preschool, before he could read! This was not that long ago. What parents of my generation consider appropriate is almost the exact opposite of what my parents' generation did. From a historical perspective, that's shocking.

So, what is culture? There are lots of definitions out there for the term. I think of it as the operating system for a group of people. It's a shared set of ideas, biases, and past experiences that add up to a way of doing things everyone takes for granted. And for the few who don't take that operating system for granted, it's the set of ideas and biases they are reacting against as they try to find their own way of doing things.

A culture forms any time a group of people comes together. Families have their own, which is why the early years of a marriage can be a huge adjustment as two people try to blend different ways of doing things that each assumes are obvious. In fact, all our groups and organizations have their own cultures, nestled into that of our larger society. That's why different workplaces, neighborhoods, schools, houses of worship, sports teams, and clubs have their own. The list goes on.

We form cultures for a very good reason: cultures give everyone a sense of what to expect and how to go about living and interacting. They offer something we want and need: a sense of belonging. But we only get to belong if we follow the rules.

Professional cultures in both Western and non-Western countries are currently obsessed with achieving peak productivity at all times. We want to optimize everything: our work performance, our fitness, our inner lives, and even our kids. That's why so many people now approach parenting as though it were a professional work task instead of a relational family experience. The ShouldStorm is a specific culture within our larger culture, stoked by this optimizing/perfectionist ethos in modern society. When I spoke about parenting in my TEDx talk, people immediately started inviting me on podcasts or to speak at their corporate events about the ShouldStorm at work.

It is virtually impossible to describe something as complex as culture change without oversimplifying, and that's a risk I run here.

A lot of factors contributed to our cultural ShouldStorm: modern technology gave us the illusion that we could fix any problem, the single-family living arrangement so common in the West isolated parents from support, and an increasingly competitive job market incited parents to optimize their children's education. Those circumstances set the stage, but it was ideas that truly started us down this path—ideas that are rooted in different moral agendas, some admirable, some debatable, and some utterly deplorable.

Old-School Parenting

Before the ShouldStorm arrived, parents were what I call "old-school," because the same parenting methods and ethos had been around for decades. Historically, children had been sources of labor on family farms or apprentices to craftspeople, and society saw them as strong, capable, and responsible for their own choices. Adults and children alike faced corporal punishment for infractions. By the mid-twentieth century children were no longer seen as sources of labor, but as people with developmental needs and wants, a view promoted by Benjamin Spock, whose first book came out in 1946. In the 1960s, Fred Rogers, like Spock, incorporated aspects of child development into his messaging and modeled an additional level of caring to postwar parents, but old habits die hard. When I was a child in the eighties, my parents, like their peers, expected me to make good decisions, solve my own problems, and spend my time outside—while also spanking me and using other shaming practices that we'll later discuss. But we had time in a way kids today don't—time to get bored and figure out what to do about it, time to ride bikes in a pack of kids, time to be out until the streetlights turned on.

Old-school parenting taught us to rely on ourselves, but it also taught us that it was weak or shameful to need help. Our parents raised us the way they were raised, often telling us to "suck it up buttercup" and "get over it and move on," and we repeated these messages to each other. We learned that we had no backup. We were taught one way to live: tough it out. But toughing it out only works up to a point. That's why when parents from my generation become exhausted from intensive parenting, we can default to the way we were raised, shouting words of shame at our own children. Then we feel incredibly guilty, which drives us to tough it out and work harder to be intensive parents.

The truly ugly side of old-school parenting was how it dealt with behavior. The goal was a well-behaved child who complied with the expectations of adults. Kids were good or bad, and infractions were punished with verbal shaming or corporal punishment. Corporal punishment was normal and most often consisted of being spanked, standing in a corner, doing manual labor, or having soap put in our mouths. Every kid I knew was spanked, just like me and my brothers. We were taught that kids who were not "whupped" ended up spoiled or sissies, a message that was reinforced by TV shows like *Little House on the Prairie*. Even parents who did not spank their kids typically employed verbal shaming. Phrases like "How could you?" and "Why can't you be more like your sister?" were used at home and at school for shaming purposes.

Shame works. It feels so bad that we will do just about anything to make the feeling go away. "The problem is that shame can be very effective in the short term in getting kids to behave. That's why it's so ubiquitous," Richard Schwartz, a doctor in Harvard Medical School's psychiatry department, told me.[11] Our own childhood experience with shame is why the ShouldStorm feels so familiar to parents and why we buy into it automatically—because we were trained to comply immediately when we are shamed.

Corporal punishment and shaming taught us to suppress our emotions in favor of compliance. "People don't really realize the consequences internally for the kid when they lead with [shame]. And those consequences include the vulnerable parts of the kid feeling worthless or bad, and then having to get away from that with some kind of extreme…activity," said Schwartz.[12] As a pediatrician, I've coached many parents through the process I've had to follow myself, of learning how to befriend parts of ourselves we learned to hate or hide as children. It can take years to unlock buried emotions, but we have to do the work because we cannot teach our own kids to regulate their emotions if the only method that we ever learned was to suppress our own. And if we fail to grapple with our own shame, as parents, we will inevitably shame the parts of our kids that resemble what was shamed in ourselves.

The Birth of Attachment Parenting

In 1975, a Manhattan socialite and model who'd had a painful relationship with her mother wrote a book about a tribe in Venezuela. Jean Liedloff had first met the Yequana tribe in the early 1950s after "jumping on the train as it was pulling out of the station" in Italy with a man she'd met at a party in Venice the night before. She eventually returned to the United States and in *The Continuum Concept*, Liedloff, who never had children, recorded her observations that the Yequana children "were responded to—without judgment—the moment they needed anything." She shared her belief that all parents should parent like the Yequana, and "that babies should be continuously carried by, and never separated from, their mothers, until such time as they are able to crawl away by themselves."[13] She advocated co-sleeping and on-demand breastfeeding.[14] For Liedloff, these parenting practices and the closeness to nature created children who were "little angels" and were "uniformly well-behaved: never fought, were never punished, always obeyed happily and instantly."[15]

So much, however, depended on the entire tribal village system in which they lived, which Liedloff didn't fold into her prescription for parenting perfection. Not an academic or anthropologist, she didn't adequately contextualize that the hunter-gatherer Yequana had a single way of living, a clear set of skills to learn, uniform expectations of child behavior, and the constant support of a village held together by generations of interrelationships. She noted, "In the jungle, every man, every woman, every child knows how to take care of babies.... Very small children are trusted to take care of infants because, five minutes ago, they were babies themselves."[16] But she failed to calculate how those attributes would complicate a cut-and-paste approach to parenting for American mothers alone in single-family homes whose children must learn abstract concepts and skills to prepare for a range of future career options.

Heavily influenced by her book, pediatrician William Sears published his first parenting book in 1982, bringing these ideas closer to (but not yet quite into) mainstream parenting literature. His book *Creative Parenting* proposed parental immersion and devotion. Sears advised mothers — specifically mothers — to be in constant physical contact with their babies via birth bonding and breastfeeding. He urged bedding close to the baby, babywearing, and "belief in the language value of your baby's cry," which means that a baby's cry is communicating something and their parents should respond immediately. These concepts, which were drawn directly from Liedloff's book, asserted that babies must never be left to cry and that a responsive mother builds a secure attachment by tending to her baby at the first moan.

While Martha Sears, a nurse and William's wife, was not a coauthor on the first book, she is credited by him with being a partner in all of his ideas and work and was a coauthor on later books in the Sears parenting library. Martha Sears has been quoted as saying,

"When Bill wrote *Creative Parenting* (1982), he referred to it as 'immersion mothering' and 'involved fathering.' At a talk one time in Pasadena, a grandmother came up to Bill and said she thought the term immersion mothering was a good one, because some moms find themselves in over their heads. When he told me of this, I realized we needed to change the term to something more positive, so we came up with AP, since the Attachment Theory literature was so well researched and documented, by John Bowlby and others."[17] Instead of questioning why mothers might find their parenting philosophy overwhelming, the Sears simply rebranded by adding a sheen of scientific credibility when they linked their untested philosophy with attachment theory and renamed their immersion mothering protocol "Attachment Parenting."[18]

Attachment theory, however, is entirely different and separate from the Searses' principles of attachment parenting. As a result, a fundamental misunderstanding about attachment theory is at the root of a lot of the anxious overparenting (or underparenting, once we burn out) that we do.

According to attachment theory, when children form secure attachments with their parents or caregivers in the early years, they can become independent adults and go through life with significantly better health and happiness. If the attachment is insecure because of inadequate parenting, or severely damaged by abusive parenting, that child will struggle as an adult. So far, this is accurate psychology. Confusion began when people had trouble deciding what adequate parenting was. Parents collectively asked, "What is good enough?"

In the 1970s and 1980s, researchers came up with hard, quantitative data to give parents a sense of what is necessary to form a secure, healthy attachment bond as understood by attachment theory. In 1986, a team led by developmental psychologist Edward Tronick found something remarkable: mothers who had secure attachments with their infants (as opposed to anxious or avoidant attachment styles) were in a matching or synchronous state with their babies 30 percent of the time. The other 70 percent of the time, these mothers were not "correctly attuned" to their infants' emotional states. During the time that the babies were out of sync with their mothers, they used their coping skills and worked to get back into sync. Thus, loving, attentive mothers—"good enough" and beyond—who have secure attachments with their kids move in and out of sync with their children and the bond stays secure.[19]

Tronick's team believed that a baby might feel bad while missing their mother's attention, but when it occurred 70 percent of the time or less, that misattunement was actually healthy practice that did not damage the relationship bond. They developed a model of mutual regulation that explained the inevitable ebbs and flows between a securely attached mother and infant. When the baby could get back into sync with the mother after a rupture, the baby had good feelings and felt an active sense of mastery and accomplishment. And those feelings of accomplishment help children build confidence.

When we parents try to get it right 100 percent of the time (which is such overkill from the necessary 30 percent), we overparent; we may get in the way of our real job as parents: to provide a safe place for our children to figure out complex relationships with real human beings. Kids need to experience frustration and disappointment with safe people who are committed to them before they face an impatient world that is not. But instead of the reasonable parenting approach Tronick's research on attachment might have prompted, the Searses offered the exhausting intensity of immersion mothering, rebranded as attachment parenting, claiming that mothers needed to be in a synchronous state with their children not 30 percent of the time, but as close to 100 percent of the time as they could get. The seed for the ShouldStorm was planted.

* * *

William and Martha Sears came to parenting from similar back-grounds: as children in the Midwest, they both attended Catholic school from kindergarten through college. William—or Bill, as he is known—even studied to be a priest, and Martha has said, "Growing up, I didn't know any non-Catholics."[20] Both had difficult child-hoods: Bill's father left the family when he was one month old; Martha recalled a home full of violence—her mother was diagnosed with schizophrenia, and her father drowned when she was four years old. The couple met at Saint Louis University Hospital where Bill was in his last year of medical school and Martha had her first job as a nurse. They married six months later and had their first child in 1967. Later they moved into the Evangelical church, right around the time that theologian George Knight III's "different but equal" argument became the church's dominant view. When Knight argued that God had instituted a permanent subordination of women to male leader-ship at home and in the church, many evangelicals concluded that a woman's place was in the home.[21]

As a new stay-at-home mother, Martha turned to what was then the only parenting book around, *Dr. Spock's Baby and Child Care.* "But when I got to the part where he says if your kid is screaming and wants to get out of the crib, don't get him, let him throw up, I said, 'I'm done with this book,'" she told *Time* magazine. As a child, Martha had been deeply affected by a relative who was a "colicky, fussy baby." Martha believed that the way "back then, they didn't know what to do with these babies, and she was just left to cry in her crib," had "damaged her brain" because this relative later developed mental illness.[22] "You could say I'm reacting to my background," Martha told *Time* about why she tells parents not to let babies cry. As a stay-at-home mother, Martha was able to make sure she didn't let her babies cry.

In 1997, Bill and Martha Sears published *The Complete Book of Christian Parenting and Child Care* for the evangelical audience. In it, they write that some "mothers choose to get back to their jobs quickly simply because they don't understand how disruptive that is to the wellbeing of their babies. So many babies in our culture are not being cared for in the way God designed, and we as a nation are paying the price."[23] More recently, the Sears have started giving advice about work-life balance, but also suggest mothers quit their jobs and borrow money to make up the difference.[24]

Beside their obvious blindness to the economic needs of the majority of moms in the United States who must work to put food on the table even while the law entitles them to a scant six weeks of maternity leave, comments like this reveal what those who attempt attachment parenting already know: it only works if mom stays home with the kids. Women who heard the insistence that mothers are the essential parents and should meet children's needs at all times perfectly or risk traumatizing the children soon realized that working moms were never going to be able to pull this off. The guilt was crushing, and it still is, because these ideas are present everywhere. Stay-at-home moms experience burnout-level pressure, while working moms live with the knowledge (false, of course) that they are failing their children every day.

The Searses claimed that attachment parenting is based on science—but it is not. They constructed their beliefs about parenting in reaction to their backgrounds, in the context of their religious and cultural beliefs, and only later claimed that their parenting philosophies were science-based. As Martha stated, they made a conscious decision to hook their system to John Bowlby's evolutionary attachment theory, but that theory did not appear in their writing in 1987.[25]

The Flawed Science of John Bowlby

John Bowlby was trained as a Freudian psychoanalyst, and in the 1950s he developed the evolutionary theory of attachment, in which he argued that children have a brief period to bond with their mothers specifically, and if they miss it they will never have the attachment they need. He based his theory on a 1935 paper by Austrian zoologist and ethnologist Konrad Lorenz, which concluded that geese (not human children) will follow the first moving thing they see. Lorenz believed that a goose was genetically programmed to attach to a single parent who happened to be there in the critical time when the gosling was between twelve and seventeen hours old and could never attach to anything else.[26] That permanent "imprinting" helped the geese survive, but it could also cause unhealthy behaviors. For instance, in 1966, a researcher named Philip Guiton got chicks to imprint on yellow rubber gloves and later found some of them trying to mate with the gloves.[27] Lorenz's theories about permanent problems for geese were further debunked by research in 1976,[28] and it is now clear that imprinting for geese is not permanent. In other words, they are able to attach to more than one caregiver in more than one small window of time.

But in 1958, when Bowlby was developing his theory of evolutionary attachment in humans, he used this bad science about geese—note, he wasn't even using research about humans—to argue that human children, like ducks and geese, attached to one primary parent, an idea known as "monotropy," and that the critical attachment window was the first two and a half years (later he claimed it was the first five years). In other words, according to his work, if kids didn't attach correctly to their mothers (and for Bowlby, as for Freud, only their mothers) during that time, they might never attach at all. Bowlby insisted that the attachment figure had to be the mother, otherwise they suffered from maternal deprivation and would experience long-term problems.[29]

Of course, Bowlby was dead wrong about how and when human children attach to caregivers. Evolutionary biologists have found that when human females evolved to stand upright, their pelvises changed to support them against gravity. Those changes also gave women more pain during labor and made them more likely to die in childbirth. In response, human infants evolved to be able to bond well with a variety of caregivers.

Adoption is an ancient human tradition found in every culture.[30] When a mother dies in childbirth, other members of their community form healthy attachments with the infant as they care for and feed them with animal milk or a wet nurse. "Though early researchers studied mothers, current research shows that fathers, co-parents, grandparents, babysitters, and even older siblings can be significant attachment figures."[31]

The Flawed Science of William and Martha Sears

Just as William and Martha Sears renamed "immersion mothering" as "attachment parenting" to lend their ideas scientific gravitas, they attempted to link science with Martha's belief that a baby's crying caused permanent brain damage. In an attempt to justify the beliefs that they already held, Bill cited a number of studies that don't actually say what he claims. One author from Yale, who was incorrectly cited by Sears, said, "It is a mis-citation of our work to support a non-scientifically justified idea."[32] Nonetheless, Bill cited her study when he claimed on his website that parents who try the cry-it-out method, even for short periods, may cause "harmful neurologic effects that may have permanent implications on the development of sections of their brain."[33] Any mother who believes this must logically stay with her baby twenty-four/seven and make sure the baby doesn't cry. If a mother has a colicky baby who cries for hours each day, she is burdened with a deep sense of failure. Sears then threatens parents that this permanent brain damage could cause behavioral problems, a lower IQ, poor school performance, antisocial behavior, or ADHD.[34] The offhand cruelty of this groundless claim is shocking to me as a pediatrician. For a doctor to accuse parents of causing their child's ADHD because they didn't comfort them well enough as babies is bad enough. But it's also just not true. Research actually supports the opposite conclusion: that babies born with the neuroatypical brains that eventually get diagnosed as ADHD cry more as infants.

The Sears parenting philosophy may be good for some, but the idea that it is the only way to a secure attachment or that it is scientifically proven is a fiction and one of the key beliefs that led to the ShouldStorm. Here is Alan Sroufe, a developmental psychologist at the Institute of Child Development at the University of Minnesota, where he and his colleagues have studied the attachment relationship for years: "Attachment is not a set of tricks. [The Sears parenting principles] are all fine things, but they're not the essential things. There is no evidence that they are predictive of a secure attachment."[35]

When John Bowlby told the world that human children might suffer for a lifetime if they did not attach to their mothers at a young age, both the early breastfeeding and natural birthing movements ran with the idea. To this day some breastfeeding and natural birth advocates who teach hospital-based prenatal classes tell expectant mothers that they will miss out on bonding with their babies if they use pain medicine in labor or don't breastfeed for several months, despite decades of research disproving this. And while the Searses had been publishing their parenting plan for years, it was only after they rebranded it as "attachment" and incorporated an exaggerated version of Bowlby's threat that they made parents anxious enough to put their books on the bestseller list.

The Searses used the same classic formula behind the get-rich-quick schemes and quick-and-easy tricks for dropping fifty pounds that fill my email spam folder. We all know it well: follow this new program with the one, right answer to succeed, or face a terrible consequence. Of course, most of us know better than to trust celebrity body sculpting with no effort, but when a pediatrician and a nurse used such tricks to sell their program, attachment parenting spread quickly and spawned all sorts of variations on intensive parenting by other authors. As a consequence, what contemporary parents assume is the level of attention children need is based on a very specific misuse of science by people with a specific set of values, not science.

Helicopter Parenting

By the 1990s, attachment parenting had become hugely popular and was a big reason for the emergence of the helicopter parent, who hovered protectively and constantly tried to cushion their children from even minor difficulties or negative emotions. At the same time, parents were newly safety-conscious, viewing the outdoors as dangerous and relying more on adult-supervised activities. Children were no longer seen as capable; rather, parents began to believe that kids were fragile and needed constant protection. Some parents proudly announced they were their kids' best friends and didn't need to set boundaries, a scenario that was lampooned in the movie *Mean Girls*. Amy Poehler's performance as the "cool mom" who had let her daughter run amok and become a narcissistic bully was both funny and painfully true. When such parents told their kids that they were the smartest, most good-looking, most special people in the whole world, they encouraged unhealthy narcissism and a fragile self-image in some kids and, more often, produced deeply insecure kids full of self-doubt.[36]

Having been raised old-school, I cannot know what it was like to be a child raised by a helicopter or cheerleader parent, but many of my patients' parents do. They tell me that they learned to suppress their emotions and unacceptable parts of themselves just as thoroughly as I did, but for a different reason. Because their parents needed them to be happy and confident, they learned to pretend that they were, even when they were not. This created shame and anxiety, and now as parents themselves, they must learn to love and accept the parts of themselves they rejected.

When it comes to attachment, Bowlby may have been wrong about when and with whom an infant bonds, but what he got right was truly revolutionary. He was able to see that human infants are born not as blank slates but are biologically programmed to form social bonds. This is important, and its import cannot be underestimated. It provides the foundation for a lot of research, theory, and thinking that has helped us understand human relationships between parents and children today. But his idea that babies must bond to their mothers in a narrow window or be messed up for life is still being circulated in the ShouldStorm.

Recently, intensive parenting has taken on a slightly different form. Now parents are under pressure to stay calm at all times and model near-perfect emotional regulation for their children. This generation was taught to suppress their emotions as children and are now told they must model emotional regulation for their children by, in effect, once again ignoring their own emotions. As Jessica Winter writes in a recent *New Yorker* review of the wave of gentle parenting books, parents must "complete a transformation into a self-renouncing, perpetually present humanoid who has nothing but time and who is programmed for nothing but calm."[37] In doing this, parents are told they can avoid traumatizing their child and that their child will learn their own emotional regulation from their model.

However, this is a distortion of the science, which we'll go into more deeply in Chapter 5. It is true that young children regulate themselves in response to their caregivers' emotional regulation, a concept called "co-regulation," and that co-regulation eventually sets the stage for a child's self-regulation. But in order to develop healthy self-regulation, children, as well as adults, must have healthy relationships with all of their emotions. If the ShouldStorm tells parents that cool calmness is the only acceptable emotion they may show and effectively forbids them from expressing a full range of human emotions when parenting, parents—and their kids—will fail. I think of it like the fraught situation in the Pixar movie *Turning Red*, where thirteen-year-old Mei Lee turns into a giant red panda whenever she feels exuberance, excitement, or anger. When her mother asks her to exile the red panda spirit (forever) because it is an "inconvenience," we see the terrible predicament for Mei Lee. There is no outlet for so much of who she is—both what makes her happy and what makes her upset. And this is precisely what current intensive parenting practices are modeling.

Fortunately, Sigh, See, Start is an emotional regulation tool. Parents can use it to stay calm, but also to engage respectfully with their own big emotions, as well as co-regulating with their children. Sigh, See, Start is also a decision-making and problem-solving tool, and its method of observing children helps parents respect their capabilities as individuals instead of invading their boundaries. In the next chapter, we'll hear from kids about their experiences, and then in Part 2 of the book, we will start using Sigh, See, Start and begin our journey to freedom from the ShouldStorm's anxiety for both ourselves and our kids.

CHAPTER 1 : KEY TAKEAWAYS

- Old-school parenting relied on corporal punishment and verbal shaming to get compliant behavior from kids.
- Old-school parents believed their children were capable and gave them more freedom than kids receive today.
- Attachment parenting was a key driver of the shift to helicopter parenting, but it was never based on science.
- Helicopter and cheerleader parents overprotect kids they see as fragile and incapable of independence.
- Whichever type of parents we had, parents today often have to learn how to self-regulate their emotions, rather than suppressing them.
- Today's intensive parenting tells parents to stay perfectly calm at all times or risk traumatizing their children.

Chapter 2

Kids in the ShouldStorm

Here's a tough thing about being a kid: when you're small you can get hurt by basically anything. It's just really hard to be a kid because you don't know what's going on. Sometimes you're confused about what's going to happen. And you just don't know what to do.

—Mason, age eight

My patients have shared so much with me over the years, and I have come to see that our children are strong, and they possess a lot of grit. But they are also under a lot of pressure and are often confused about what's expected of them. The incompatible demands of the ShouldStorm that push parents to alternate between rescuing their children from minor difficulties and then also insisting on the highest achievement, for example, can be stressful and contribute to a child's anxiety or depression over time.

In this chapter, we consider a handful of stories about kids to look at what we often can't see in our everyday lives: how the ShouldStorm can disconnect parents from what we could see with our own eyes and keeps us working overtime in ways that may interfere with, rather than support, our children's development as secure, confident people. These are just a handful of stories, but each speaks to a situation I have heard time and again.

Most of these stories come from interviews with volunteers in the parenting group I facilitate, and some are a composite of children I have seen over the years. The group is diverse in their genders and races, but they all came from suburbs, towns, or city neighborhoods considered safe places to live with good schools. Their stories are their own and cannot be assumed to speak for any other children, and yet they illustrate themes and experiences that are common in this generation.

The stories and what I have learned from kids may be surprising. The shame, confusion, and intense pressure to succeed that run through these stories are not the fault of the parents alone—though parents no doubt may feel that way. Parents do communicate messages from the ShouldStorm to kids, of course, but we are not the whole story. We are but one (essential) part. The better we can see ourselves with our children and also see our children where they may be, the better chance we have to build them up.

Philip and Parental Shame

My first patient one morning was Philip, a sweet and seemingly quiet seven-year-old boy. His mother was a stay-at-home parent who wanted to talk about concerns from Philip's teachers. They had told her that he didn't talk in class. He didn't engage during group discussions and he took several minutes to join group activities. I learned that there were twenty-seven kids in his first-grade class, and at any given moment there was a lot of activity in the room. I could see that Philip was a perfectly thriving child with what many pediatricians call a slow-to-warm temperament, but I could also see that his mother was distressingly worried and even ashamed. The ShouldStorm is always looking to place blame on parents, and any deviation from a perceived ideal is not just a problem but shameful.

"He's always been shy," his mom said, looking away from me as she talked. "I stayed home with him and didn't put him in preschool until he was four. It's my fault. I tried to do playdates and story time at the library, but I should have done more."

She did what parents do: we blame ourselves. I smiled, allowing for a quiet moment before sharing my thoughts with her.

"I'm noticing something about Philip," I said. "We've been talking this whole time, and he's sitting there, listening to everything we say."

She glanced at him and smiled. "He's very observant," she said.

"I bet he's a clear thinker too," I said.

She nodded, still smiling. "He comes out with these amazing comments sometimes, like he's an adult!"

It was clear that she delighted in some of her son's strengths, but the ShouldStorm took her attention away from what really counts—often what we can see with our own eyes—and preoccupied her with the fear that she was messing up her child somehow. It is common for the ShouldStorm to tell us that what an expert, a teacher, a book, or even a mean social media comment says is potentially more accurate or valuable than what we think. The thought that we may harm our children is so terrifying that we look to the experts for instructions: What should we do not to mess things up?

Philip's teachers told his mother he should be talking more, and she accepted that it was a problem and the fault was hers. But when she and I observed Philip together, she could see a fuller picture of Philip's behavior: He talked with his teachers one-on-one, as well as with one or two other children, but not in larger settings. In full group settings, Philip wasn't zoning out or removed; he was quiet and attentive. He had a keen and observant mind. That wider picture—outside of a lens of shame and blame—helped his mother see her son and his needs in the classroom better. Sigh, See, and Start (which we were briefly doing during this session) brings the values, experiences, and intuition of the parent back on board. With this foundation, the parent is in a more stable place from which to make informed decisions for their child—not perfect decisions, because those are the things of ShouldStorm fantasies—but reasonable, informed ones by the person who knows and loves their child.

I ended my session with Philip's mother that day assuring her that Philip's quiet presence in school was not caused by her staying home with him as a baby and tending to him. She was relieved when I explained that Philip naturally had a slow-to-warm temperament and there was nothing wrong with him. Temperament is something we are born with, and every temperament has its own difficulties and strengths. The source of her shame was our society's overvaluation of extroverts over introverts, and I suggested she read the book *Quiet* by Susan Cain, one that the parents of many sensitive and shy folks appreciate. Cain's book highlights the value of these traits and offers strategies to help when those traits are not valued or don't match up with teachers' expectations. I also recommended she have a conversation with Philip's teachers about how best to support him in small and large group settings, since he is a capable and intelligent but shy child. There's no shame in that.

The ShouldStorm operates like a bad boss who you can never please because it spins on the axis of shame and false expectations. It tells us if our kids are less than perfectly happy, or if they deviate from the developmental or school performance checklist, the parents are to blame. Parents absorb that shame, and it drives them to work harder to find the right things they should be doing to "fix" their kid. Even when their child does not need fixing, like Philip. He did not need to be fixed so much as understood or seen for his particular strengths and needs and then responded to accordingly.

Chloe and Parental Anxiety

"We are just doing our homework," said Chloe's mother as she leaned over her eight-year-old daughter's shoulder. I was pulling up the patient chart on the computer.

"Ah!" said her daughter, slamming her pencil down on her paper, "This is too hard. I just can't get this."

"Don't get frustrated, sweetie," said her mom. "Let me take a look." Her mother took the pencil and paper onto her own lap, and she began writing. As I watched, Chloe's mom proceeded to finish the worksheet, occasionally saying, "See, it's like this." She seemed completely unaware of Chloe's defeated posture next to her.

Later, when I moved to check Chloe's lungs, her mother jumped between us and wiped Chloe's nose with a tissue.

"Sorry about that. She has so much mucus! It's disgusting," said her mom.

When we were wrapping up the visit, Chloe fastened the Velcro straps on her shoes.

"Let me fix those," said her mom, bending down and undoing the straps.

"Mom, I can do it," Chloe protested.

"She never gets them tight enough," her mother told me, shaking her head and tightening the straps. "Chloe, you know that you could trip and get badly hurt if you don't do your straps right."

"Is there anything else before we finish for today?" I asked.

"I've been wanting to talk with you about Chloe's anxiety," said her mother. "She lacks confidence and gets worried about the littlest things. I think I'm burning out. I'm just so exhausted from helping her with all the anxiety; it's emotionally draining."

Whether she recognized it or not, Chloe's mother had become intrusive. Rather than supporting her daughter with her homework, her efforts to help actually undermined her daughter. Like so many parents, she was acting on the ShouldStorm's threat that if she didn't protect Chloe from frustration and anxiety, Chloe could be messed up…for life! Lynn Lyons, a therapist and coauthor of *Anxious Kids, Anxious Parents*, told the *Atlantic*, "The worse that the numbers get about our kids' mental health—the more anxiety, depression, and suicide increase—the more fearful parents become. The more fearful parents become, the more they continue to do the things that are inadvertently contributing to these problems."[38] By taking over and not allowing Chloe to grapple with a bit of anxiety when doing her homework, Chloe's mother sent a message that Chloe couldn't handle it or do it, and potentially made Chloe more anxious.

The more ShouldStorm-based fear that parents feel, the more distracted and disconnected they become, and the more they can miss the impact of all their "helping." Chloe's mom could not see that she was intruding on Chloe, making Chloe feel anxious by criticizing the way Chloe did little things, and then shaming her by complaining about her to the doctor. Research shows that overparenting—that is parents who try to "help" or control everything that happens to their child—derails a child's development, leading to the very anxiety parents intend to prevent.[39]

Psychologist Madeline Levine explains the difference between support and intrusion by saying that "support is about the needs of the child, intrusion is about the needs of the parent." She argues that parents who intrude, rather than support, do so because they lack frustration tolerance; in other words, they can't handle the way their child's anxiety or frustration makes them feel, so they exert control and intrude to make themselves feel better.[40]

I agree that overparenters may lack frustration tolerance, but I differ with Levine about why. I believe that parents love their kids so much that when the parenting culture tells them they should not tolerate their child's frustration, but instead should soothe it instantly, they respond. They respond out of love and fear. The ShouldStorm messaging about soothing and relieving discomfort instantaneously begins in the infant period, with all the misunderstanding about attachment parenting and theory (which we dive into in the next chapter), and parents just keep going with it as the child ages. Thus, I would argue that support is about the needs of the child, and intrusion is about the parent's effort to keep up with the shoulds. A parent doing their child's homework may seem extreme, but it's amazingly common. The ShouldStorm tells parents to take responsibility for their child's experience instead of equipping their child to take responsibility for themselves, and many parents feel they have no other option.

Overparenters could benefit from two things: first, a more accurate understanding of what their child truly needs, and second, the coping skills to sit with the possible internal discomfort those needs may induce. With these tools, they will be able to resist helping too much. This is exactly what Sigh, See, Start gives parents. When parents learn how to use Sigh, See, Start to manage the fear-mongering ShouldStorm, they are able to engage with their kids' positive and negative emotions; they no longer inadvertently teach their kids to avoid or suppress negative emotions. And in doing so, they teach their children how to engage with the full range of their own emotions. By staying present with their children's negative emotions, parents help their children move into a more regulated state. (Self-regulation means that children learn to manage their positive and negative emotions without being dominated by them, and it's a key building block of healthy development.) Sigh, See, and Start helps parents do all of this without becoming overwhelmed themselves.

Mason, Caden, Maddie, and Unsupervised Time

As a child in the 1980s, I roamed the neighborhood with friends. My experience of friendship happened mainly out of doors and outside of school. In almost every culture in human history children spent their childhood roaming and playing, and that's where they learned physical, social, and emotional skills. In the United States in the 2020s, however, very few kids are allowed freedom to roam outdoors beyond the watchful eyes of adults. And much of kids' experience of being outside with each other now occurs during school at outdoor recess, which in my school district means about fifteen minutes a day, if the weather permits. With such a short amount of time to play with friends after so much sitting still and focusing, it's no surprise that the play at recess can get a bit out of hand. The kids' bodies have a developmentally encoded instinct that tells them to go, play hard, climb high, and challenge themselves to see what they can do. But this puts them at odds with the ShouldStorm influenced safety-consciousness of the ever-watching adults.

———

Eight-year-old Mason has felt bad about himself for years because of the way his energy level gets him in trouble. A bright, caring child, Mason worries about the way his body urges him to move or talk in class. "I see his internal struggle," said his mother, Lindsay. "I feel like he masks it at school, and then he comes home and he's just done." She worried about the way Mason often identified himself as a bad kid. What Mason needed was regular ample blocks of time to wiggle and express his enthusiasm. Mason did get movement breaks at school, but one or two minutes here and there did not meet his body's needs.

By telling a young child that his need to move was a problem to be solved, we'd put Mason at odds with his own body and made him feel ashamed. And the worst part is that all the sitting and focusing is not good for any of our kids: their physical health, metabolism, ability to focus, social development, and emotional wellbeing would be much better if they had the hour and a half of recess I had as a kid in public school. The ShouldStorm's emphasis on academic optimization is costing our kids.

Mason was confused when he got into trouble at recess for playing with snow one day. "I was just playing with friends, and we were throwing snow and then we got in trouble. We didn't know that it was not right. It wasn't hard snow, and we weren't throwing it at anyone," Mason told me. He said it made him feel "weird, confused, and guilty" and told me he finds it very hard when adults have inconsistent rules. Mason has just identified something important: confusion triggers shame. When he was told that the harmless play his body naturally prompted him to do was wrong, it put him at odds with his own body. When the natural and non-harmful needs of their bodies are wrong, kids feel humiliated and incompetent because they can't make sense of the adult rules that go against their every instinct.

I am certainly not criticizing Mason's recess monitors. Many parents hold schools responsible for making sure kids don't get hurt at all. Many kids enter kindergarten after years in professional daycare centers, where parents receive a phone call and must sign an "incident report" if their child sustains the slightest scratch or bruise. In my pediatric office, I have counseled many parents who want to switch daycares because they found a tiny bruise on their child but did not receive an incident report. They felt the daycare was neglectful because no one prevented it or even saw it happen. My best efforts at reassuring them that such minor bruises are a healthy sign that their child is exploring and learning physical skills with their bodies do not console them. If that's what parents expect, how can any public school allow the kind of freewheeling physical fun kids need?

One area that has also suffered because of so much adult supervision is a sense of self-reliance and independence. Time and again, I hear about the trouble children have learning how to resolve conflict when an adult is not present. So much is learned with the help of adults, of course, and such help is also necessary to keep kids safe in instances of bullying or antisocial behavior. Often, though, a parent's stories about bullies make little sense to their children today because the rules have completely changed. Their parents were taught that the only way to get a bully to stop was to hit them back, or preferably to win a fight. But now it is commonplace for the kid who hits back in self-defense to get the harsher punishment from their school principal. Kids are taught nonviolence and to tell a teacher if another child is hurting them or teasing them. The adults are the ones expected to intervene. Nonviolence is, of course, good and necessary, but the problem comes when the all-or-nothing tendency of the ShouldStorm renders a child confused or powerless to defend themselves when necessary.

————

Caden started having nightmares and anxiety symptoms after another first-grade boy sat on his chest and choked his neck on the playground at recess. His mother found out when the principal called her at work, praising Caden's nonviolent response and pointing out that Caden was a "good" kid. She was incredulous; their elementary school was highly ranked and considered very safe. At least her son wasn't violent or a troublemaker.

When she asked Caden about what had happened, he was visibly frightened and unclear on the timeline. He didn't want to talk about it, but he did indicate that the other child had been choking him for "a long time" and did not stop until another kid went to get a recess monitor.

After a week when Caden's nightmares worsened despite his parents' attempts to comfort him, Caden's mom and dad sat down with him. During their conversation, his parents were stunned to realize that Caden had believed that any form of self-defense could get him in trouble at school. "I knew they were telling them to get a teacher instead of hitting back, but I never thought he'd feel he wasn't allowed to protect himself at all," said his mother.

His parents were in full agreement. They clearly and directly gave him permission to hit back or defend himself if someone was hurting him and he couldn't get a teacher. Caden didn't believe them at first, but they promised in no uncertain terms to back him up with the principal or the police or anyone else. "When he realized we meant it, Caden's mood got better instantly," said his mother. "He went from walking around hunched over to standing up straight. He slept through the night that night."

Over the years, the principal called a few more times. Every time, he praised Caden as a good boy who didn't use violence but asked the teachers for help. Caden never had to take his parents up on their permission to hit back; simply knowing he was allowed to protect his own body was enough. His parents' response helped because they truly saw and heard him, and gave him action steps that specifically met his needs in the situation he faced.

Caden is only one of many boys and girls I've known with similar stories, who were given such a strong message about not hitting, which of course is a good thing, that they did not know they had a fundamental human right to defend their own body. By overdoing the message that adults should always be the ones to protect kids and never the kids themselves, kids may actually feel less safe because they know that the adults can't always be there.

———

Maddie was having trouble with some of the girls from another school on her fourth- and fifth-grade recreational league basketball team. The first time a girl slapped her, Maddie felt confused and asked herself why. Another time during practice Maddie was going for the ball and accidentally slapped the hand of one of the girls. "She kind of dropped the ball and then she started slapping me and I said, 'Why are you slapping me? You saw me. It was on accident.'" After that the girls started saying mean things to her, pushing her, and hitting her with the ball. The coach never noticed because bullying happens when adults aren't looking.

Maddie tried avoiding the girls or getting away when they used the ball to hit her. "I was trying not to hit her back. I just kind of knocked the ball out of her hand and then I went away." But it never occurred to Maddie to talk with her coach or her mother. "I mean, it made me feel pretty bad," Maddie told me. Maddie was feeling embarrassed and ashamed, a perfectly normal response to violence or aggression. And like so many kids who are bullied, Maddie shut down. After all, who wants to draw attention to something so humiliating?

Eventually Maddie's mother found out, but only after Maddie said she didn't want to go to basketball anymore. They talked it through and came up with a plan, given that there were only two or three games left in the season. First, Maddie would talk to the coach, which she conceded might be helpful. If the coach was not around to help, she said, "My mom told me that if they hit me, I tell them to stop. If they continue doing it, I hit back. But I do not like to hit people, so if they're hitting me with their hand, I can put the ball up. That gets them away from me, and I don't have to hit anybody."

Maddie's mother found a nonaggressive way for Maddie to assert herself and feel safer. (If it got really bad, she promised, Maddie would quit the team.) Just like Caden, Maddie needed permission to defend her body, but because of her abhorrence of violence, what helped her was a plan for nonviolent resistance. What Sigh, See, Start helps parents do is see what their specific child needs; it helps parents see a more expansive or accurate picture of themselves and the child and proceed from there.

Grace, Kaleb, and Adolescent Pressure

The COVID-19 pandemic profoundly affected kids' sense of safety, their home lives, and the way they were schooled. This is the kind of formative experience that will impact the way our children approach their lives and adulthood, much the way wars have impacted prior generations. What that impact will be, both positive and negative, is something we can only understand over time. And even before this huge crisis took a sledgehammer to the mental health of so many of our kids, many adolescents were facing a crisis of anxiety and depression. One major contributor is an unforgiving sense of pressure to succeed, driven by a need for control over the insecure and increasingly unsafe-feeling larger world and the insecure economic and political futures of us all.

As reported in the *Washington Post* in 2019, America's National Academies of Sciences, Engineering, and Medicine added a surprising group to their list of at-risk youths. Along with children whose parents were incarcerated, who were in foster care, or who were living in poverty, they added children attending "high-achieving schools." These children were designated at-risk for mental and physical health problems caused by chronic stress. The Robert Wood Johnson Foundation had reported the same concern a year before in 2018, pointing out that "excessive pressure to excel" belonged among poverty, trauma, and discrimination as one of the top environmental factors that harms adolescent health.[41]

———

Grace was a perfect daughter. An excellent student at a highly ranked public school in an affluent suburb of Chicago, Grace brought home report cards filled with As, and her parents never had to remind her to get her schoolwork done. She played the cello in her high school orchestra and the advanced string ensemble, was an officer in her school's National Honor Society, and did volunteer work, as well as other activities. Even better, Grace was a help to her parents in caring for her younger sister with special needs. In a word, Grace was the ShouldStorm's ideal teenager.

But it came at a cost. During her annual physical when she was sixteen, Grace answered the routine screening questions for depression in the positive. When her mother left the room so Grace could talk with me, she poured out her heart. "My parents have to work so hard to take care of my sister, so I try not to cause them any trouble," Grace told me. She made sure to perform well in school and during her activities. But ever since middle school, she had been privately suffering from painful anxiety.

"It used to be just a lot of anxiety, but since I started high school, I think I've been depressed," Grace said. And it was getting worse: for the past few months she hadn't been sleeping well, she had little appetite, her grades had dropped slightly because she was finding it hard to concentrate, and she constantly felt like she was letting her family down. When I asked her whether she thought about hurting herself, she looked at the floor. "Yes. I try not to think about it, but the thoughts just come," Grace told me.

She had learned about depression in health class, and knew she needed to talk to someone, but was afraid to tell her parents how she felt. Grace explained that her parents had immigrated to the United States in adulthood, and their upbringing had not given them an understanding of mental health, so they viewed anxiety or depression as a phase that would pass, or as a weakness to hide.

I've heard this story from kids of every background, whether their families had lived in America for generations or were recent arrivals from all over the world. And many of those kids told me they hid emotions not for cultural reasons, but because their parents always got so upset if they were sad. They were protecting their parents from their emotions by toughing it out on their own. For decades, pundits and experts have accused kids, teens, and young adults of being "wimps" who can't handle anything because they've been coddled by parents, teachers, and coaches.[42] But in my experience, there are a lot of kids who have the opposite problem: they don't know when to quit being tough.

Grace was preparing a perfect résumé to get into a top college, following what kids are told is the path to a successful life. What Grace, and her parents, did not know is that it doesn't matter what college she goes to. High school grades don't predict future success very well, and the Pew Research Center has found that people's "feelings of personal satisfaction and economic well-being are about the same, no matter which type of institution they attended" for college.[43]

Psychologist William Stixrud, who describes himself as a mediocre student who flunked out of graduate school before he found his way in life, wrote an article in 2018 for *Time* magazine called, "It's Time to Tell Your Kids It Doesn't Matter Where They Go to College." In a wonderful illustration of what kids are being told, Stixrud calls out our shared delusion "that the path to success is narrow and you'd better not take one false step." He identifies untrue stories our kids are hearing that foster fear and competition: that you have to get into an Ivy League school to succeed in business, or that screwing up one time in high school will impact the rest of your life. "This false paradigm affects high-achieving kids, for whom a rigid view of the path to success creates unnecessary anxiety, and low-achieving kids, many of whom conclude at a young age that they will never be successful and adopt a 'why try at all?' attitude," he writes. All of this leads to unhealthy self-talk, where kids tell themselves, "I have to, but I can't," or "I have to, but I hate it."[44]

By following the high achievers' script, Grace had disappeared behind her own achievements and missed out on the key developmental task of her adolescence: discovering a sense of self. Because who she really was or what she liked or disliked were irrelevant to her performance, at the age of sixteen Grace was already facing the emptiness of her life, a treadmill of hard work and top performance extending endlessly into her future. What did she have to look forward to? If she worked very hard in high school, she might have the chance to work very hard in college, and then in graduate school, which would give her the chance to work extremely hard in a high-performance job. And now Grace was ashamed that she couldn't maintain that top performance.

The saddest part of the story may be that Grace once loved learning, but a focus on achievement had crushed that love. Research shows that this is an international problem. In one paper, researchers looked at fifty countries and noticed that when the national culture promoted high math achievement it killed the students' interest in math. And in a fascinating twist, students in countries with lower math achievement scores showed far more interest in math. Both effects were more prominent in girls.[45]

But Grace was facing another struggle. Much as Mason suffered confusion and shame when he was criticized for following his natural instincts to play with snow, Grace was confused and ashamed of an instinct she barely understood. In order to produce her top grades, Grace was denying the natural and unavoidable imperative of adolescence: exploring who she really was. Psychologist Madeleine Levine was thinking about kids like Grace when she wrote,

Kids can't find the time, both literal and psychological, to linger in internal exploration; a necessary precursor to a well-developed sense of self. Fantasies, daydreaming, thinking about oneself and one's future, even just "chilling" are critical processes in self-development and cannot be hurried.[46]

Grace needed time and freedom to have long conversations with her friends, but they were also high achievers with no time to hang out. She needed time to daydream, or mess around and waste some time, or try an activity she wasn't good at, preferably in an informal setting. But first, I had to convince her parents to get her to see a therapist without delay.

Therapy is one of the most useful tools we have as parents, and like so many treatments, it is most effective when used early, before problems become deeply entrenched. Unfortunately, many parents have gotten the message that if their child needs to talk with a psychologist, it's because they've failed them. This is simply not true: the more we understand how hard growing up has gotten for kids, the more we can see that parents cannot and should not need to go it alone. We all need support, and therapy can be our first line of defense against serious mental illness in our kids: the earlier we help them this way when they struggle, the earlier they find new ways to thrive.

* * *

When the ShouldStorm in adolescence is focused on achieving life success, it introduces a surprising and harmful should: Find your passion. Teenagers are led to believe that if they find their passion, they can follow it to a fulfilling and lucrative job, and thus a happy life. Finding that passion and pursuing it with grit is the path to salvation from the woes of what is now an insecure and highly competitive working world where only a few people achieve financial success, and even fewer seem to be doing jobs they love.

Teenagers likely hear this message from their teachers and parents, and then the media they consume reiterates it. And like most other shoulds in the ShouldStorm, being told to find their passion actually interferes with what teens need to be doing developmentally: freely exploring without worrying what it means. Fifteen-year-old Kaleb feels a lot of pressure when he's told to find his passion:

> We don't know what adult life truly is. We just don't know. I feel like if I make the wrong decision, am I going to be stuck like this for the rest of my life? I have this little panic attack, like what do I want to do? Am I going to mess up? Am I going to choose the wrong thing?… And I feel like all the choices and decisions coming at us are like missiles, and it's really hard to dodge…. You're figuring out who you are to get to the gateway into adulthood. I feel like the gate is made out of barbed wires.

Purvi Mody, a college admissions expert, writes about the day she recognized the question "What is your passion?" was "too heavy to ask a young teenager—that asking them actually did the opposite of inspire, it made them feel like they were behind others, like they were somehow failing the college admissions race because they were still discovering themselves."[47] She echoes many experts in adolescent development when she urges parents to ask a different set of questions, including "What inspires you?" and "What do you want to learn about?"

She goes on, "These days we are so focused on the end goal—getting kids into a certain college or on a path to a successful career…. But if we really stop and look at those around us, what we see is that people who are truly successful and happy took a winding path."

The research backs this up, as David Epstein meticulously documented in his book *Range: Why Generalists Triumph in a Specialized World*.[48] In it, he shows the productive benefits of what many might call inefficiency.

As parents, we would do well to listen to our kids' insights. At the end of our interview, Kaleb told me, "It's not if I choose the wrong thing. It's just, I chose this and I don't like it. I'm going to try something else. The world is a lot of maybes." He certainly feels the pressure, but Kaleb has already recognized something many teens don't: that he can change course even as an adult. This generation is capable of profound perspectives. I am stunned, almost daily, by the wise words of our kids and the way that they observe their world and the adults close to them. "Life is like a staircase," Kaleb told me. "You can't get to the top of the staircase and find out what you're doing without all the little steps."

In the next chapter, we'll learn how to use Sigh, See, Start to connect with our kids where they are and meet their genuine needs.

CHAPTER 2 : KEY TAKEAWAYS

- Parents are sometimes told that good features of their child's personality are a problem, simply because they don't fit a specific mold.
- Kids don't need to be fixed so much as seen and understood for their particular strengths and needs.
- Kids need parents to support their development, not to intrude by helping too much (even if well-meaning).
- A lack of physical activity in schools is hard on kids and increases anxiety.
- Kids need permission to defend their own bodies, but they need to do this in a way that works for them.
- The pressure to achieve drives anxiety and even depression in kids.
- Too much time spent achieving gets in the way of other important developmental tasks.
- Therapy is a first line of defense when kids are anxious or struggling.
- Truly successful people often take a winding path, and kids do well to explore rather than worry about finding their passions.

PART 2

EMERGING FROM THE SHOULDSTORM WITH SIGH, SEE, START

Chapter 3

How to Use Sigh, See, Start

I feel like I'm unlearning so much of what I learned as a kid.
—Jennie on using the Sigh, See, Start method

It's changed everything. It's completely changed our home.
—Marisol on using the Sigh, See, Start method

Sigh, See, Start is a method to help you gain clarity and confidence for your parenting. If you've read a lot of parenting books—and I have—you may be used to specific instructions to address common parenting problems. The instructions make sense, but the overwhelming amount of detail makes them almost impossible to follow. In the heat of the moment with your child you can't or don't do it precisely as instructed (because real life is more varied than simplified scenarios); so, you end up yelling, waffling, messing up—or doing fine—but you feel worse. You know there's a specific way you should be handling this situation, and you've failed. You may become overwhelmed by your self-criticism, guilt, or confusion. And in moments like these, Sigh, See, Start can be an antidote. It can help you find your strength and clarity. And from this more confident place, you are better able to apply all the wisdom, love, motivation, and knowledge that you have about yourself and your children. You can and will make parenting choices and decisions that work for your family. I know it sounds a bit unbelievable, but it works.

How to use Sigh, See, Start

———

Sigh: When you feel confused, overwhelmed, or unsure of what to do—in other words, when you are being driven by a storm of conflicting shoulds—do this: Sigh, take a deep breath, all the way into your belly, and then let it go long and slow. Imagine it's a sigh of relief. Sighs help you stop going down whatever negative path you may be on and center yourself, allowing you the opportunity not to be bullied by the should in your head.

———

See: Observe your child. See if they look happy. See if they are close to tears. See if their fists are balled in anger. Take in the information that is in front of you and nothing more. You are not yet at the start phase, so you are not analyzing; you are not planning or assessing. You are observing and collecting information that may be useful. When we skip this stage, we often see only what we expect to see and not all that is truly there—or not there!

———

Start: Then (and only then) start thinking about what may be appropriate in that very moment. Could a hug help? Could they use some space? Do they need a minute to accept a limit you just set? Do they need to figure it out for themselves? Start by trying something different, or even just pausing and doing nothing. What you do may or may not work, but the most important part is to start; that is how you will learn more about your child. When you notice and recall what works and what doesn't, you unleash the true power of Sigh,

See, Start. The more you start—whether what you do is successful or unsuccessful—the more you learn. At first, making mistakes may trigger shame that you should have done things differently, but you can simply Sigh, See, Start again. Mistakes are no longer something to fear, but an essential part of the learning process.

———

The method is so simple that at first it may seem like another too-easy answer. I doubted it myself when I first came up with it, but then I saw how it worked in parents' lives and I knew it was a lot more than a simplistic answer—it requires us to grow and change. And the power of Sigh, See, Start is in the practice of it: when we commit to using it, we find it hard to avoid growing as a parent. These steps can be applied to any situation and to any parent, no matter how impossible they may think change will be, and it can work. Marisol, a self-described perfectionist who is "wound pretty tight" and pulled in many directions, put her doubts aside when she watched my TEDx talk and started using the method that same day. And within hours, she saw the benefits.

What Does It Mean to Say Sigh, See, Start Is Working?

When I say something is working, I mean it is transforming our relationship with ourselves and with our kids; it is helping to create greater trust, understanding, and respectful collaboration. Yes, you can be the one in charge *and* collaborate with a three-year-old, as we'll learn more about in Chapter 7. Fortunately, this approach has the added side effect of improving our kids' behavior, as well as our own.

Since one of the best ways we learn is through examples, in this chapter I'll share the stories parents have told me, and the lessons we have learned about how to use Sigh, See, Start. These examples are illustrations of how real-life parents customize the method to their family and their needs. When they use Sigh, See, Start, they are

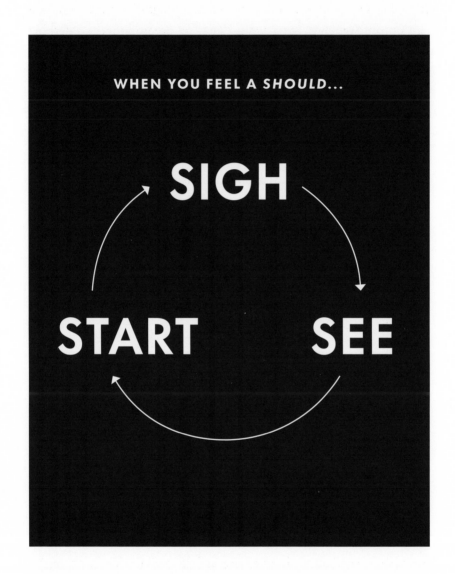

THE THREE-STEP METHOD:

SIGH

*Take a deep breath
and let it go long and slow.*

SEE

*See your child.
See the situation.*

START

Start trying something different.

(Start something, start nothing, start
the wrong thing; it doesn't matter because
each time you use Sigh, See, Start
you will learn more about your child.)

not following a prescribed should technique to cut and paste into their lives. My hope is that you will be able to see bits and pieces of yourself in their processes and be inspired to think about how you and your family could use the method. By the time you are done with this chapter, you will have a clear sense of how to use Sigh, See, Start with your own kids.

SIGH

———

Take a deep breath all the way into your belly. Like a sigh of relief. The sigh is our body's built-in mechanism for pulling us out of the fight-or-flight centers in the autonomic nervous system that show up for us as anxiety. We will discuss the science and physiological processes that occur when we sigh in Chapter 5, but when we sigh and breathe deep into our bodies, we connect to ourselves differently than before; and when we breathe out slowly, we become present and centered, creating a calmer place from which to see things clearly.

Sighing resets our mood. Al has been using Sigh, See, Start since his daughters were infants, and finds that when he sighs, the rest flows from there. After one busy day when everyone was overtired and both Al and his wife hadn't had a chance to eat dinner, four-year-old Gracie would not go to bed. "Gracie already tries her best to stall at bedtime," Al told me. So, when Gracie started whining at the top of the stairs, Al's wife, Rachel, went up to put her back to bed. "Ten minutes later, Rachel went back up and put her to bed a little more sternly," said Al. "Fifteen minutes later, just as we started to eat, we could hear Gracie crying in her bed and as Rachel and I met eyes, she said, 'Your turn!'"

Using Sigh, See, Start has taught Al to pay attention to his own mood. "As I went up the stairs…I wasn't angry, but I was fed up with this child's stubbornness to just admit she was tired and close her eyes. So, before I even walked in the room, I stopped and sighed a few times. I knew the way I would have come across wouldn't have helped anyone. I stood outside her room just taking deep breaths and getting my mood in the right place." It was while he paused outside her room that Al heard Gracie's "deep and genuinely sad cries."

Sighing not only helped Al feel calmer and less rushed, but it also created a moment for Al to naturally observe (i.e., see) that Gracie was truly upset. "I asked Gracie what was going on and it was, 'I miss Mommy. I'm not tired. I'm sad. I want to play.' The usuals!" But because Al had sighed into a calm state, he did not react right away. And this next pause gave him a chance to hear what Gracie said next, "I prayed for God to make me feel better and to help me not be sad, but I still feel sad." Al was touched. "My eyes were leaking…. So, I sat there with her, and we took deep breaths together. I taught her about counting sheep, and I scratched her back." Al explained to Gracie that he wanted her to use breathing and counting sheep to put herself to sleep and then he left the room. She fell asleep shortly afterward.

Parents with tough sleepers know that they can get lucky one night and the self-soothing lessons may not stick the next night. But the overall approach of connection and supporting what the child can do themselves, repeated over time, can lead to gradual improvement with a difficult sleeper. By hearing Gracie and connecting with her, Al was able to comfort and set a limit, reinforcing their family goal that Gracie soothe herself to sleep. Even better, the next day Gracie was still processing what Al had taught her the night before, something parents find happens more often when they use Sigh, See, Start. "Gracie told Rachel about what we talked about and how she felt better," said Al. Later when Al got home from work and they were playing together, Gracie recapped what she had learned the night before with him. When we interact with our kids from the connected place sighing brings us to, our kids are much more likely to take the lessons we give them to heart.

Sighing can be difficult, but stick with it anyway. Sighing is not always easy, particularly for action-oriented parents like Jennie. "I am somebody who wants to respond quickly," she shared with me during one of our parent coaching sessions. "I am inclined to want to find the right answer, give it to them, and move on. My brain goes right to a solution that's worked for me," she said, expressing her impatience with times when what works for her doesn't work for her kids. Jennie is pointing out something that most parents experience at some point.

Making decisions quickly and taking action are a strategy that has worked well for Jennie, both in her childhood as the oldest of four children and in the adult workplace. When we've found a strategy that works for us, we tend to use it everywhere, even when it doesn't serve us. "I have dealt with coworkers who talk so slowly that it drives me crazy....I have a really hard time waiting for them to finish their thoughts....I just want to go ahead and keep moving.... Let's just get to the answer."

So, it's no surprise that when Jennie first learned about Sigh, See, Start, she skipped straight to the seeing step. To Jennie, sighing felt unnatural, and she found it awkward that "there's something to do before the action; it's hard to just stop and deliberately do [nothing] with my body." And because Jennie was already getting results by using seeing before her usual jump-in-and-start approach, she didn't understand why I thought sighing was so important.

One thing I had observed with Jennie during our parent coaching sessions, as I have observed with most other parents, is that whenever she described a challenge she was having with one of her kids, she led with analysis. She had already thought through the situation analytically and reached conclusions about what was going on with her kids, as we all do. But her kids were often unreceptive to Jennie's solutions. Have you ever shared a personal problem with someone, looking to be heard and understood, but instead they dropped their conclusions and solutions on you? It can be irritating and disappointing. Like us, our kids need to be listened to and understood, not just talked to or at.

Sighing often reveals our blind spots. Leading with her strength as a problem-solver helped Jennie a lot, but many times it also created tension with her fifteen-year-old son, Kaleb. She could have benefited from a different approach, but what? Kaleb often felt overwhelmed by his homework load and activities. Usually, Jennie was annoyed by it and offered an analytical solution—set a timer for each task to make sure you get it done by bedtime—and expected everyone to move on, because homework and chores are nonnegotiables. Kaleb responded just as you might expect a teenager to respond—slammed doors, anger, and the silent treatment. Lately, Kaleb has been exceptionally busy with his school musical rehearsals, in addition to his usual homework and chores. Because Jennie was using the see step, she observed that he was feeling particularly stressed and upset, and though she was consistent in her expectations for his homework and chores to be completed regardless, she felt that "there were several days where I needed to be a little kinder." Her usual directive style was provoking Kaleb to have meltdowns, and Jennie could see that he was overwhelmed. She also started to "feel like I have been a bit dismissive [of Kaleb's feelings]."

When reflecting on her own childhood and how her feelings were routinely dismissed, Jennie told me, "There's a pattern there that I feel like I've learned. It's rude to be dismissive of anyone, though. Regardless of how stupid you think their issues are." The more Jennie practiced seeing Kaleb, the more she realized that she wanted to start respecting how he was feeling—while also expecting him to do what she felt were his necessary responsibilities, such as his chores and homework. The question was how to change the tone of their fraught interactions.

And this is where sighing came in. It was only by sighing that Jenny shifted from her analytical, action-oriented mind to her heart. Kaleb, like his mother, is quite capable of getting a lot done; he didn't need her scheduling advice so much as he needed her sympathy to give him the boost he needed.

One evening, when Kaleb was yelling at her about how he need-ed to stay up past his bedtime so that he could have a moment—just a moment!—to relax and chat with his friends online, Jennie took a big, deep sigh. This time she did not say that it was past his bed-time—end of story. She sighed again and sat down, unsure of what to say or do. But she wanted to say something. As a mother of three, Jennie knew what it felt like to be worn out.

"I can empathize with you," is what she said. She could see that he looked burnt out. She felt a twinge of connection, knowing how awful she feels when she is overwhelmed and worried she may not be able to get it all done. "I can see how worn out you are."

Kaleb's whole posture changed, even as he continued to tell her that he hadn't had a chance that afternoon to see his friends.

"But you want to do [the musical], right?" Jennie asked. "You are working through something hard, and it sucks. These are long days. They are hard…. But you made a commitment. You're going to be thankful you pushed through this. It forms the resilience that makes us good at life." In this connected moment, after he had felt heard by her, Jennie found he was listening for the first time to what she had been trying to tell him for weeks about persevering when things are hard if they are also important. And amazingly, even though he still wanted to hang out with his friends online, he took his mother's next statement with a good attitude.

"You're still going to bed at 9:30, Sweetie. Your body needs this in order to function tomorrow. Seeing how tired you are, I know that this is the support you need from me as your parent."

He didn't necessarily like her advice or limits, but he respected them because she was clearly taking him in and respecting him; she wasn't giving him lip service or pushing him along. She was seeing and accepting his fatigue as something real and important. Being heard and empathized with by a mother who was truly present with him allowed Kaleb to accept her advice and her limits.

In this case, we can see that by sighing (rather than jumping straight to seeing and starting), Jennie was able to slow down enough to truly see Kaleb and herself. And then she was able to return to the start step with better information than she would have had otherwise. Until she did that, she was not really seeing her kids; rather, she was noticing a version of them that fit conclusions she already had. Think of the process as a filter for information that prioritizes details that are in service of her fix-it ways and ignores details that she may not understand or know what to do with right away.

Another parent or another family might have taken what they learned with Sigh, See, Start and then approached the start differently—and they would have been equally correct. They might have let their child skip his chores during the rehearsals or made some other adjustment to teach a lesson about time management or self-compassion. Or they might have gone deeper by using a technique for solving problems collaboratively, ahead of time, that we'll learn in Chapter 7. There are as many possibilities for what can work with our kids as there are kids; you as the parent can find a way that works best for you and your family at that time.

So, are there no "wrong" and "right" decisions or ways to apply Sigh, See, Start? Within a range, there is a spectrum of "right," so long as it fits the needs of this child and this family. What is that range? The health and safety of the child and family members must remain intact, of course; and as the research taught us with attachment theory, kids need us to be in tune with them about 30 percent of the time. In the midst of difficult parenting decisions, we do our best, and then at some point later, it's valuable to reflect back on the moment to learn or review. When we reflect, we can ask ourselves two questions: Are we connecting with our child from the heart? And are we showing them respect as a capable and unique individual and listening to their perspective? I have found in my own home that when I use love and respect as my guideposts, I make better parenting decisions.

Kids' Problems Are Just as Big as Adults' Problems

As we develop during childhood and into adulthood, we face problems that strain us to the edge of our capacity. Even though they may seem small to us, the problems of a child are large relative to their developmental stage. That means that to a child or adolescent their problems are just as big as an adult's problems. It's easy for parents to overlook this and to repeat what they heard themselves as children: "You think that's hard, just wait until you are an adult and have to deal with paying taxes and a mortgage." But dismissing a problem that your child is struggling to manage doesn't help them manage the problem or put the problem into perspective; rather, it shames them and potentially increases their anxiety about becoming an adult. Does this mean that your child overreacting about a Lego is truly a large problem? No! But it can help us authentically extend kindness in the face of their meltdown, as well as an effective solution for helping everyone move forward.

Jennie recognized that sighing was the key to one of her most important goals as a parent: teaching her children grit while also teaching them empathy and emotional resilience. Until Sigh, See,

Start, she could not see how to combine these seemingly opposing values based on her own experience. Jennie had been raised old-school and faced a lot of shaming, and when she became a parent, she was determined to raise her own children differently, with more mutual respect and communication. As a result, her kids were very empathetic and had great EQ, but she was now seeing that they lacked some of the independence that she wanted for them, as well as grit. Jennie wanted to give her sons the emotional processing and awareness that she had struggled to learn as an adult, while also teaching them the resilience that has served her well and helped her a lot. When she was able to sigh and connect with herself, she finally saw a new way.

SEE

Observe your child and the situation. When we let go of our assumptions and really see our child and the situation, we are practicing mindfulness. Many people think mindfulness means having a meditation practice, which is why so many busy parents feel that it's out of reach. But mindfulness is really just engaging with the present with awareness and full acceptance.

Mindful acceptance does not mean that we put up with anything, or don't take action, or that we don't judge our children's behavior as acceptable or unacceptable. It means that we accept the reality in front of us. We don't try to change it right away. We don't pretend people aren't feeling the way they're feeling. We accept it as it is before we act. For those of us who live our lives in the ShouldStorm, acceptance can be both surprisingly difficult and surprisingly freeing.

Some people think of mindfulness as mental awareness, but I believe that true mindfulness includes our presence. In other words, mindfulness in parenting means being present with your kid and with yourself. And that's why sighing before you try to see your child is so important, because the act of sighing pulls us into our bodies and helps us become present.

See what you didn't see before. When Alecia told me during a parent coaching session about the struggle she was having with her oldest son, Noah, age eight, she led with her analytical mind, just like Jennie. But, when I asked Alecia to sigh with me, she reacted very differently. She began to cry.

"Your mother's heart is coming to the surface. You just love your child," I said.

"It feels overwhelming, the sadness, if I stop and sit too long."

Alecia is pointing to a common strategy that parents—particularly, mothers—use to survive the ShouldStorm: to outrun the overwhelming anxiety and burnout that our culture of anxiety creates by staying busy mentally and in activity for our children. Most of the time, Alecia felt powerless to help. Noah would be distressed and tell her about kids being mean to him, but it often sounded like he misinterpreted something or was leaving something out. It always sounded off enough that she didn't understand what was wrong (outside of his obvious and heartfelt distress). One day, she was present for an incident and she was able to use Sigh, See, Start to navigate the moment.

"It was at a picnic at the beginning of the year for everyone in the third-grade class to get to know each other. Everyone is at a picnic, and he's sulking by himself. He was upset that I was late, and then he was saying that he tried to play soccer with these kids and they didn't kick the ball to him and nobody wants to play with him. But then, a friend came over to us and said, 'Noah, do you want to come collect acorns with us? We're collecting acorns.' He turns to her and says, 'No! I don't want to.' Then, turns back to me and continues about how no one wants to play with him," said Alecia.

She sat next to him on the bench, rubbing his back, but he rebuffed everything she said about trying again with the soccer kids. Here he was, yet again, angry, removed, and convinced (somewhat oddly) that no one wanted to play with him.

So, she sighed, just as we had practiced during our session. In the sighs, she noticed that a part of her was feeling big feelings of shame (*Why are all the other kids playing so happily and he can't?*), anger (*Noah is way overreacting!*), and confusion (*What should I do?*). She sighed again and again, while rubbing his back, not knowing what else to do. Since she was only at the sigh step, I was proud that all she was doing was breathing and bringing her awareness to herself and her body, without judgment. In the past, she would have been mad at herself for feeling angry or being confused. But today, in the park she was becoming aware of her feelings and letting them be, rather than overwhelming herself with trying to ignore them or fight them. And in this presence, she was able to open up to the next step: seeing anew. She sighed into her uncomfortable feelings as she rubbed his back; she was feeling embarrassed, but she was acknowledging and managing those feelings, rather than being dominated by them. Organically, she began to see new details: some girls sat next to them on the bench and started eating their snack.

"Are you hungry?" Alecia asked. He nodded vigorously. It turned out lots of kids were eating their snacks, but Noah had forgotten his. Once she gave him a granola bar from her bag, he softened. A lot. He let himself be pulled into a conversation with the snacking kids sitting nearby, who had been trying to engage him earlier. When it was time to go, he gave her a hug.

Alecia didn't consider this much of a victory, but I reminded her that one way kids with sensitive nervous systems can try to manage the world is by becoming rigid about routines and inflexible about surprises or change (hence, the big reaction to her five minutes of lateness). And because such children can react so strongly, parents often become frustrated with the hard time they are having. In this small moment, turning his isolation around so that he could join the picnic was indeed a win.

But this was just the beginning of Alecia's new way of seeing things. Once you start seeing, you can't stop seeing more links and connections. A few days later, the teacher called to say that Noah was so exhausted in school that he put his head down on the desk during math (his strongest subject). Alecia went back into a shame spiral (Why was there always something wrong with her kid? Something other parents could probably handle?) and worry: She had been spending hours with Noah every night trying to get him to sleep, and he just could not or would not fall asleep. She rubbed his back, she read to him, and she lay next to him, but he just wouldn't fall asleep. The night before, after scratching his back for a long while, she left him to read until whenever he fell asleep. Which turned out to be midnight.

After the phone call, she sighed, and instead of being overcome by her usual shame self-talk, she made note of it. She noticed her discomfort, and suddenly, something clicked: when not distracted by her own feelings of inadequacy, she could see Noah more clearly. She could see that he was tired and hungry during these incidents, and, given the highly sensitive child that he was, his threshold for overstimulation was low as a result. Possibly, he was often overstimulated. It was an aha moment. Instead of stalling in shame and only considering how she was at fault or how she needed to change how she was parenting, she began to think anew about what would help him with his overstimulation and those specific things that were difficult in the moment. If he's hungry, then he needs to eat more. And if he's tired, then he needs to sleep more. What they were doing now, as reasonable and thoughtful as it was, wasn't working. Noah often skipped meals he didn't like, so Alecia let go of her should about nutrition for the time being. Instead of varying his meals, she let him eat yogurt smoothies for breakfast and packed him mini pizzas for lunch, day in and day out. Regarding Noah's desperate need to sleep, Alecia had long resisted melatonin, but she finally took her pediatrician's advice and gave him the recommended gummies until he was better rested and then they could reevaluate. She went hard on the practical and soft on the shoulds and the shame to get to a place that might help reduce instances of overstimulation and give him more bandwidth generally.

After just a few days, not even a full week, of Noah getting a full night's sleep (ten hours in his case) and having a breakfast, snack, and predictable lunch that he liked, his teacher called to say he was like a new person. He was playing at recess; he was engaged during class. He was almost totally changed. And, most surprisingly for Alecia, the stories about the kids being cruel also seemed to change. Once Noah was better regulated and resourced, he was able to see that so much of what happened in the day was not a direct rejection of him, as he previously had been interpreting it. Alecia was delighted. And she felt proud of herself for trying out things that helped him get the rest and nourishment he needed so that his school days turned around dramatically.

* * *

Seeing allows for grace and compassion. Alecia, like so many moms, had an intense inner critic, but prioritizing her son's needs over her shoulds required her to replace some of her inflexible judgements with a little compassion. Her self-talk became kinder. Sure, she told herself, her solution was not Instagram pretty (no lush blackberries in a ceramic bowl) nor as healthy as what she gave him before (which he wasn't eating anyway), but she got him what he needed, and that felt good!

At our follow-up session, Alecia told me about the picnic, the call from the teacher, and her more-food-more-sleep start plan.

"Looking back at the picnic, maybe my 'fault'—being late—wasn't the only factor in his struggle that day. Maybe I wasn't so horrific and the cause of it all? Maybe in the scheme of things I was good enough, and just life was happening, and he could use a snack."

I absolutely agreed. This was the first time during the pandemic that the kids had really played together without masks on. Excitement is very stimulating, and when that is coupled with hunger and disappointment, it can be physically stressful. Noah is a sensitive child, and he had reached his limit. His state of overstimulation left him without enough bandwidth to be patient when he tried to join the soccer game. What she saw probably was unhealthy rumination when he removed himself, but it was also a natural way to decrease stimulation.

Everyone has different sensory thresholds. Most of us (about 80 percent) have nervous systems that notice a normal amount of sensory input. But about 20 percent of us have nervous systems that pick up on and process everything, from sights to sounds to smells to physical sensations to emotional and social input. This gives us a talent for noticing details others might miss and can lead to some deep creative thinking—and, indeed, Noah was a highly intelligent child, who made observations and connections that served him well in his schoolwork—but can also lead to becoming more easily exhausted or over-stimulated.[49] And when people are overstimulated their nervous systems react by trying to decrease all stimulation—because even fun or a hug can feel like too much, and can even feel almost painful. That's why when your child is really upset they might react like you are hurting them if you try to hug them. Most parents quickly learn to wait until their child has calmed down to offer that hug, but underestimate the role that stimulation plays.

By using Sigh, See, Start, Alecia parented in a way that worked better for both herself (more self-compassion) and for Noah (getting fed) rather than the way that she thought she should (never taking the easy way out and encouraging Noah to eat a variety of foods at lunch). Alecia trusted that the time would come when she could start growing Noah's range of foods. Given the nature of Noah's worries and sleeplessness, Alecia had wisely gotten the number of a child therapist, but the change in his whole being was so remarkable that she held off, knowing it was an option they might want to use at some point.

Parenting is full of foggy days and confusing moments, and engaging with that means we are really in it with our kids. Since our kids are not projects to be managed or problems to be solved but are interesting and complicated little people who often don't know how to articulate how they feel or what's going on with them, staying in it with them is what they need most from us.

Seeing our child can be a lot of fun. Sigh, See, Start doesn't always mean digging deep. It can be quite a lot of fun and very playful, as Marisol discovered. Like that of many four-year-olds, her son's play could be frustrating, and he often ignored her commands to stop it. "I kept trying [Sigh, See, Start] and I started to be able to notice what he was doing and think, 'He's a four-year-old.'"

Marisol kept at it, taking deep breaths and observing her child, and she intuitively became curious about what in the world it was like to be a four-year-old. So, during one of the times that she used sighing, and then seeing, instead of trying to cast about for what she thought might or might not be going on with her son in that moment, she asked him directly. "When he was throwing his toys I asked, 'Why are you throwing your toys?' and he said, 'I'm flying them.'" That gave her an idea of how to start. "I suggested something else to fly." It was a win for both of them: Her son was just as happy flying the rolled-up socks she gave him, and Marisol didn't have to worry about property damage. But something much more important was also going on in that brief interaction. By respectfully asking her son about his play, Marisol modeled good relationship skills. When she was present to him in openness and curiosity, she made her son feel valued and understood, building his trust in her.

Marisol initially had trouble generating ideas for what to start with her son, because as a great student in the classes she was taking, she had been trained to look for the "right" answer. But as a student she had also learned to stay curious. To switch from her strength at finding what she should do (an excellent habit for an ultrasonographer who should do medical imaging the right way), she had to sigh her way out of anxiety. "I know you said it was for parenting, but I've applied it to anxiety," Marisol confessed to me. Sighing allowed her to transition to curiosity and see what was going on. And part of what she could see was an individual who happened to be a young child. When Marisol mindfully acknowledged that her four-year-old son might be experiencing his world very differently from the way she experienced it, even if they were sharing the same space, Marisol unlocked something magical. She asked him questions with genuine curiosity and without any tone in her voice that suggested an agenda, and her son opened up and gave her all the information she needed.

* * *

See helps us engage with our children at their developmental stage.

Marisol wasn't the only mom who found it helpful to see from a child's perspective—I did too. On one family vacation, we were sure our kids would be as delighted by NASA's Kennedy Space Center as my husband and I were. Instead, they drove us crazy with complaints, and my frustrated husband and I began talking about how ungrateful our kids were and rapidly approaching anger.

That's when I hid in the restroom and did Sigh, See, Start by myself. When I sighed, I recognized that the ingratitude I was hearing from my kids was simply the way I was interpreting their behavior. Suddenly I remembered what it had been like to be a kid on a family vacation: the excitement and then the letdown when something turned out to be boring, my achy legs and back at museums when my dad wanted to read every exhibit, the yucky feeling of having to behave when I wanted to run and climb.

So, I replayed my memories of the day and tried simply to see my kids' behavior. "I strongly believe that behavior is communication," my kids' elementary school student services coordinator, Elly Goldstein, always liked to say. Not only had my kids clearly communicated excitement followed by disappointment and boredom, but they'd been tortured all day by seeing ice cream and gift shops every three yards and constantly being told no. It was obvious that the next thing to start was something they would find fun.

When I returned from the restroom, I could hear my kids' giggles. They were climbing on an amazing play gym while my husband sighed in relief. I sat down next to him.

"You know, they've been telling us that they needed this all day," I said, "we just weren't listening."

"At least we got to see a space shuttle," he grinned.

START

——

Try something new. As you may have noticed in the examples in this chapter so far, start grows directly from your presence (sigh) and observations (see). Therefore, your start will be highly tailored to you and your family. And so, it's worth noting that starting is hard— but powerful—because you are trusting the connection, presence, and knowledge that you bring.

As parents, we long to know what to do so we can offer our best to our children, but we have so little faith in ourselves that we fail to recognize that it's less about what we do and more about how we do it. When we bring our presence and compassionate attention to our children, we have already started giving them what children need most. In fact, it's the longing for that genuine connection with us that lies behind so many of our children's annoying attention-getting behaviors. Just think about how good it can be simply to spend time with someone you love: there is something renewing and even healing in that. And that's what we can start giving our children by sighing and seeing.

Start modeling for your kids. Start is all about taking the information we've gathered and engaging with the creative process. Parents who don't think of themselves as creative can just call it problem-solving with better information. And this is where Sigh, See, Start begins to look very different from other parenting techniques.

The more you use the process of Sigh, See, Start, the more you change. Each success both teaches you new information and grows your confidence, and each mistake also teaches you new information for learning, until you find solutions.

Because starting challenges you to trust your own problem-solving, it can trigger your inner critic when you first begin using the method. Each time that voice in your head tells you that you've failed, or that you should have done things differently, Sigh, See, Start again. Sometimes, you'll recognize the need to seek repair with your child, something we'll look at more deeply in the next chapter. More often, you'll recognize the ShouldStorm talking, and rather than ruminating or getting defensive, you'll find it gets easier to ignore it as you use Sigh, See, Start to tackle the problem from a different angle. This unique approach to mistakes, rolling them into a process of growth, is an incredible tool to model for your children.

As we saw in Chapter 2, kids face their own ShouldStorm, fanning anxiety about being good enough. Most parents have heard the saying "Kids do what we do, not what we say," but may not realize just how true this is. Modeling is one of the most powerful ways kids, and all mammals, learn behavior. Watching and learning what our parents model is part of the social learning that is critical for survival, and large areas of the brain are devoted to it.[50] And unlike learning through rewards and consequences, when kids learn through imitating what they see us do, they develop a sense of agency as they control their own learning. If we can show our kids a way of being that is engaged, honest, and flexible, we are teaching them resilience. And by modeling self-regulation, presence, mindfulness, and an open and respectful approach to problem-solving, we are equipping them with skills for life.

When Al's oldest daughter was three years old, she would pull him into a "daily courtroom" to "plead her case," as he put it. It was both cute and irritating, and Al found that sighing helped him resist his knee-jerk instinct to assign blame in this daily charade. Instead, he'd ask her questions and try to see what was upsetting her, by asking, "What's going on here?" Then he started modeling respectful listening and problem-solving, eventually with both his daughters. It really paid off: now that his daughters are two and four years old, he frequently hears them working out their own arguments without him. "Of course, if someone hits her sister in the head and it's automatic tears, I have to go and intervene, but I think the process is there."

Start is about reinforcing the process of growth, in yourself and your kids. Sometimes not everything lands at first, but this process is one that builds on itself and grows with time.

Overparenting and Start

Overparenting is at the heart of a lot of ShouldStorm parenting. Fear driven and action- and goal-oriented parents step in and do things for their kids in a way that interferes with their children's growth—such as doing a child's homework for them instead of supporting them through the stress of it. When parents are first using Sigh, See, Start, I encourage them to consider starting to step back a bit more, both by taking time to see—to observe before you start — and by starting to let kids do things for themselves, even when they struggle. According to research from the 1980s, even at six months old babies internalize their own learning experiences if parents were quiet enough to let them.

When you start, some of these suggestions may be helpful

→ *Use information generated directly from your observations.* Alecia was able to reset her son's behavior by giving him a snack when she noticed he was hungry. Parents of a newborn can relax when they observe that their baby simply needs to cry sometimes, even after they've done everything they can to comfort the child.

→ *Ask your kids for ideas.* Because our culture tells us that parents should know what to do and direct their kids, we simply don't think to ask our kids for their thoughts. We'll look more deeply at how to collaborate with our kids in problem-solving in later chapters, but I've found just the right thing to start countless times by simply asking my kids, even when they were only three years old.

→ *Engage their imaginations and playfulness.* Marisol encouraged her son's imaginative play of "flying things" by substituting a softer object to throw. I got my own sons past their anxiety about riding their bikes to a nearby friend's house by turning it into an "adventure of exploration," complete with a printed map of the route and little boxes of raisins in their backpacks for "provisions."

→ *Avoid battles.* Not everything has to be a power struggle. In fact, common power struggles have been found to impede child development. Examples include power struggles in potty training that lead kids to start withholding and develop constipation, or with food, where research shows urging young eaters to eat may create picky eaters. (Parents control what, where, and when kids can eat; the child controls whether and how much.)

→ *Step back or adjust your involvement.* Let the kids work out their own arguments. Have you ever noticed the way your kids try to involve you as a referee whenever they are arguing? So often you end up in a dissatisfying back-and-forth and no one is happy with your decision.

→ *Let your child work through their own frustration.* Whether they are a two-month-old practicing lifting their head on their tummy or a twelve-year-old struggling through their homework, frustration is a useful motivator for kids to achieve their goals. Try not to rescue them from frustration because you may take away their chance to have a victory, but do provide support and encouragement, and do comfort them when they melt down or shut down because no learning is happening then.

→ *Teach your kids Sigh, See, Start.* Try teaching school-age kids how to use it so they can benefit from the self-regulation, mindfulness, and confident approach you've learned.

→ *Allow for natural consequences.* Instead of preemptively setting a rule or punishment, allow the situation to play out (within, as always, safe boundaries). At the beach, we told my son not to leave his sandwich unattended. He didn't listen. Instead of packing it for him, we left it and a seagull ate it. He was upset, but it worked. After he (and I) sat with his feelings, he said, "I can't believe I let the seagull get my sandwich." A moment later he repeated it. When he opened his animal crackers, we didn't have to hound him and he didn't leave them unattended.

→ *Apologize when there's hurt between you and your child.* When you make the kind of mistake that causes hurt, own it. Take full responsibility and apologize. Repair is an essential part of the parenting relationship, which we'll look at more closely in the next chapter.

* * *

Sigh, See, Start is a journey toward connection with our own difficult feelings as much as with our children's. And it happens moment by moment, issue by issue, accumulating over time. Raising kids is not a set of individual problems to solve, one after the next, in isolation and with right answers. Raising kids is a journey fraught with emotions—theirs and ours.

Sigh, See, Start is a decision-making tool; an emotional regulation tool; a brain reset tool that helps us shift out of old patterns; a mindful practice; an executive function booster; and a complementary practice to any parenting style or therapeutic strategy.

Chapter 4

What You Won't Get from Sigh, See, Start

We're killing ourselves, trying to be perfect, and it's making us insane.

—Amy in the movie *Bad Moms*

Every day, parents in my office tell me how much they want to be perfect and how guilty they feel that they are not. It's amazing how often parents use the word *perfect* when they talk about their parenting goals. They don't say *good* or *loving* or *adequate*; no, when parents think of their kids, they want to be perfect for them. Other parents, like Cheryl in the story that follows, would never use the word perfect, but they might use the word *right*. They want to get it right or do the right thing. And this is true even when parents know full well that the complexity of life is beyond a straightforward right and wrong. Whether parents use the words *perfect* or *right*, they are talking from the perspective of life in our high-pressure parenting culture, where there is no room for doubt or trying our best.

When I ask parents what perfect looks like, they usually refer to their desire to meet their kids' needs ideally and instantly. A perfect parent, they tell me, is always attuned to their child: synced up with their child's moods and reading their cues, anticipating their emotional and physical needs and able to help.

Yet, as silly as it seems to use an impossible standard like perfect or right, at a deep and almost unconscious level, parents have come to believe that perfect is what kids need. And using perfect as the standard makes every single parent a failure.

Sigh, See, Start will never make you a perfect parent.

Sigh, See, Start works because it rejects the idea that perfect parenting is the goal. The method is designed to help parents build our confidence because it focuses on what we are learning and how we are growing, rather than on our mistakes. Sigh, See, Start is all about stepping out of old patterns and creating new ones, so it can help parents who never had safety from their own parents create loving and safe relationships with their own kids or help parents find footing in totally new and uncomfortable times.

Thank goodness our kids have us, in all our humanity and with all of our mistakes. Loving caregivers provide something no one else can. Family is a place where we can annoy each other and work things out with people who are committed to our welfare. Kids get to practice the hard stuff with those who love them and provide for them, before they go out into a world that offers no such commitments to them.

Taylor was a bright fourteen-year-old student who did well in school and was always full of interesting things to talk about. But Taylor had also been struggling with anxiety for years, and they were now in a depression. Their mother, Cheryl, told me she wasn't sure what to do anymore, and so here they were in my office.

I asked if I could talk with Taylor alone, and that was when Taylor told me to call them Taylor—even though that was not the name given to them at birth and not the name their mother called them—and that their preferred pronouns were they/them.

"Don't call me Taylor in front of my parents," they said. "But you can use 'they' in front of my mom."

"Does your mom know how you feel about your gender?" I asked.

"Yeah, she knows," said Taylor.

Taylor and I chatted, and they agreed that we could talk with their mother about their gender identity, but today I would keep the name Taylor between us while using the pronoun *them*.

When Cheryl joined us, she explained to me that she very much wanted to support Taylor, but she was confused. She didn't know whether the way Taylor was dressing was a phase or a deeper part of their identity. She felt like she should know the right way to talk to Taylor, but didn't know where to start, so she didn't say anything at all. She was worried about Taylor's sadness.

Cheryl was in completely new territory on many levels—parenting a teen and addressing questions of gender that she had never had herself. And like so many other parents, she was caught in a ShouldStorm of self-doubt and worry. She was distracted by trying to figure out what she should do and was thus missing out on connecting with her child.

"Let's try Sigh, See, Start," I said. We all sighed deeply, and I asked Taylor and their mother to make eye contact and really see one another. Each gave the other a soft, tentative smile. Then, I asked Cheryl to start telling her child what was in her heart.

Cheryl started by telling Taylor that she loved them more than anything. And Cheryl said that she was worried about how much harder life might be for them dressing as they did. She didn't want life to be harder than it already was. I could tell Cheryl felt embarrassed by these fears and her thinking, but whether she liked it or not, it was there, and it was interfering with her ability to connect with her child.

Taylor then demonstrated something I've seen again and again in my practice, particularly with gay or gender nonconforming kids: they had tremendous generosity toward their parents. To my surprise, Taylor said they didn't expect their mother to get it, but Taylor valued their mother's effort. It mattered that their mother loved them and wanted Taylor to know they were loved.

And that simple love between a parent and child is what the ShouldStorm has a way of obscuring with all its demands. It told Cheryl, you should know what to say. You should know what not to say. You should do this or that. But when Cheryl tried Sigh, See, Start for the first time, it took her just moments to turn her attention away from the should and be vulnerable and brave to give Taylor what they needed most: love and connection.

The two of them decided that they would start to go to a therapist together. In the visits that followed, I saw much more confidence and trust between them.

Sigh, See, Start helps us engage with our kids when we are confused and overwhelmed. When we sigh into our bodies and become present, see our child, ourselves, and the situation as they are, and then start interacting, we create a meaningful connection with our kids, which can lead to new possibilities.

Taylor does not need Cheryl to be a perfect mother. In their journey, Taylor will have to face many people who are well-meaning and confused about their gender and make mistakes. And Taylor will face those who bear prejudice against them or even hate them for exploring their gender identity. From a developmental perspective, struggling through the process of communicating about this with their loving and committed mother can be a growth experience for Taylor that strengthens them as they face the outside world.

And that outside world is a ShouldStorm that is constantly telling Taylor how they should be and why they are wrong for being different. It turns out that when Cheryl shared her uncertainty and vulnerability and grappled with her personal parenting uncertainty right in front of Taylor, she gave Taylor an important opportunity to practice dealing with the same. And when Cheryl used Sigh, See, Start to reconnect with Taylor, she showed them how to restore what matters most.

In our culture, the image of the perfect parent is held up for us to admire, even as that image shames us with our own failure. But what would happen if that perfect parent actually existed? Let's imagine what it would be like to be raised by a truly perfect parent. For the purposes of this exercise, let's imagine a mother, because parenting culture has traditionally emphasized the role of the mother.

Imagine you're a child with this perfect mother. You are small and imperfect and you make mistakes. But she doesn't. You smack your sibling and pull their hair, and your mother never loses her poise. When you need something, she seems to know what it is, always. So much so that she often understands you without your even needing to explain anything.

As you go through your childhood, your mother's perfect ability to meet your needs in the moment means that you never have a chance to feel really bad or experience a full range of human emotions or face the challenge of having to figure out what to do when your mom doesn't meet your needs. Inside, you feel a growing sense of inadequacy and you dread the day that you have to be an adult and try to do things for yourself. Do you see the problem? Parental perfection takes away our kids' space for child development.

We are raised by human parents so we can learn how to be human among other humans. Sigh, See, Start can't make us perfect parents, but it can help us give them something even more important.

Rupture and Repair

We can and do hurt our kids, and sometimes we can hurt them badly. But repair is an amazing thing when it comes from our heart. Most of the time, when we make mistakes or cause minor hurts, we repair them in the course of our time together. Sometimes we can hurt our kids more deeply, by shaming them or being unavailable when it really matters.

There is a large body of research on ruptures—small daily frustrations and disappointments, as well as larger scale ones—between parents and kids, and the research says that they are natural. It is not possible for people who live together who all have different pressures, goals, and wants not to end up in conflict with each other at times. Your two-year-old wants to throw the spaghetti on the newly painted wall because it makes an awesome splat sound and the sauce drips artistically. You want the paint to survive a week before it's damaged. And because you are tired and have been working hard, you yell loudly at your child to get them to stop. They cry, and you have a rupture.

The science says that the way you create a secure attachment with your child is through those ruptures and—crucially—the repairs, not through helicopter parenting. As Diana Divecha writes about the work of researcher Edward Tronick, whom we met back in Chapter 1, "Life is a series of mismatches, miscommunications, and misattunements that are quickly repaired…and then again become miscoordinated and stressful, and again are repaired. This occurs thousands of times in a day, and millions of times over a year."[51]

This constant practice with stress in relationships is how kids build their skills, and it is how parents build healthy attachments with their children. That's why the ShouldStorm's warped view on how attachment is built is so toxic. It turns what the actual science says 180 degrees, claiming we must keep everything smooth and easy for our kids and avoid their feeling frustration and stress. When we listen to our culture and do this, we undermine the very attachment we are trying to build.

Conflict is so normal in human relationships that the research shows the closer you are with someone, the more conflict you have with them. For instance, kids have more conflict with friends than they do with kids who are not their friends, and siblings argue constantly.[52] Further, conflict in a couple (which goes way up as soon as a couple has kids) is described by scientists as a "normative process that has the potential to help a couple move forward adaptively by restoring balance within the relationship when the differences between partners are addressed."[53] In other words, the relationship skills of a couple can actually grow through the normal process of conflict.

Clearly, a conflict-free existence means not having meaningful relationships at all, and that is not an option for parents. But the research also finds again and again that what matters is how we repair the ruptures that come up. That's something with which Sigh, See, Start can really help.

Apologizing

Apologizing, whether we do it and how we do it, may be one of the most important ways we teach our children what we expect of them. An open and honest apology is a powerful statement of our humanity and of grace. However, the only way we will have a chance to teach our kids this is if we make mistakes that require us to apologize.

A study of twenty-four parents in Canada found that apologies strengthened the parent-child relationship. This was particularly true when it was not just the parents who apologized, but also the kids. Since kids learn how to apologize from their parents, this meant that parents providing the example was important.[54]

But the prospect of apologizing, really apologizing, can feel humiliating or stressful. And since so many of us were raised by parents who never apologized for fear it would decrease their authority, we have not had great examples of how to do it. Let's try Sigh, See, Start.

APOLOGIZING WITH SIGH, SEE, START

SIGH

Center into your body and use the outbreath to blow your embarrassment away. Keep sighing until you feel calmer about the mistake you made.

SEE

Try to see the situation from your child's perspective. Sometimes it can help to see the situation from how you might have felt as a child. This is important to help you express the apology in an authentic way.

START

A great apology says, I did this, and it was wrong. I imagine it made you feel bad or mad or sad. You matter to me because I love you so much, and that means the way I made you feel matters to me. I love you and I want to repair the distance between us. I hope you will forgive me and that we can go back to the trust and love we were feeling before, but I know you might need to share more of your upset feelings before that is possible. Then listen to your child.

It was natural and reasonable that Cheryl was anxious about saying the "right" or "wrong" thing to Taylor and running the risk of a rupture in their relationship. But, in trying to avoid harm, her silence hurt her child. An open apology expresses love, trust, and courage. The courage to take full ownership of our failure, with the belief that we are strong enough to do this. It expresses trust in our child, that we are safe enough with them to make ourselves vulnerable in this way. It expresses trust in ourselves, that we are people of character who will learn from this and grow. A genuine apology expresses love and respect in a way that no amount of perfect good behavior can, because it lays us bare before our children.

As parents, we must give ourselves the space to say, "I screwed up," without minimizing or deflecting it. When we do, we can learn how to do better next time. And we give our kids space to mess up and recover when they do. When I think about the big mistakes I've made, the times I've been really hurtful toward my children, I feel shame and fear. But then I think of the love and repair between us, and I feel redemption. I feel somehow more loved, and loving, than I did before I failed, and so proud of my children's ability to be generous toward me. I experience my children's faith in me, and it makes me feel more confident that I can be the parent they think I am. As an ancient saying goes, "There is no fear in love. But perfect love drives out fear."

In unhealthy families, all or part of the child's individuality is denied. Sometimes the child's depression or anxiety is ignored because the parent doesn't believe in depression and thinks it's a sign of weakness. Or the child is told they can't be feeling what they feel, or they need to try harder to get over it. This deepens the child's suffering because they've been told that it's their fault and their struggle is shameful. Often the child does not receive help until they have been suffering for many years and the problems have become deeply rooted. Sometimes they are never given help at all.

Helicopter parents who are devoted to helping their kids with their feelings can also teach their child that they are not allowed to feel what they are feeling. Driven by our culture's false ideas about attachment, a parent may think they are being loving by asking their child about every feeling and attempting to soothe them instantly. But as the child gets older, they understand that their parent simply cannot handle their most distressing feelings. When the message is sent that the child must never be upset, the child hears, "Don't cry." Helicopter parents often have a hard time admitting that their children are suffering, because that would be a sign that they failed to meet their emotional needs. These children frequently do not receive help until they have struggled for years.

Our goal is to help build families that are healthy, and that means repairing our relationships when we make mistakes. But what if after a terrible mistake and an apology, something with our kids has gone very wrong? Sometimes repairing relationships means taking full responsibility for ourselves by seeking help through family therapy. It is a gift to our children to show them that we are not doomed to continue in hurtful behavior, but can admit our struggles, find help, and grow. I believe strongly in post-traumatic growth and have seen people overcome and thrive after the worst that life can bring. If people who get the right support can end up happy even after horribly abusive childhoods, then parents can have hope that their families can recover from mistakes or adversity.

Sigh, See, Start will not make you a perfect parent. It will not make you suddenly able to stay calm and wise all the time. But by taking you out of the pressure of the ShouldStorm, Sigh, See, Start meets you where you are—whether you are full of patience and energy or have had it up to here—and supports your connection. You may not be a perfect parent, but you will sigh and see your way into starting your best. And that is exactly the example your kids need.

CHAPTER 4 : KEY TAKEAWAYS

- There is no such thing as a perfect parent; uncertainty comes with the territory.
- Kids don't need perfect parents; they need to be raised by real humans who model how to deal with mistakes.
- Healthy attachment is built through the process of rupture and repair.
- True repair means taking responsibility for ourselves, genuinely apologizing, listening to our children's thoughts and feelings to restore trust, and seeking outside help when we need it.

Chapter 5

The Science of Sigh, See, Start

With modern parts atop old ones, the brain is like an iPod built around an eight-track cassette player.
—Sharon Begley, "In Our Messy, Reptilian Brains," *Newsweek*

The premise of Sigh, See, Start from a neuroscience and psychology point of view is that we have everything we need to be good enough and even wonderful parents. Our bodies are full of healthy natural rhythms and signals that get derailed and misunderstood by the too-busy, modern lives we've built. Reconnecting to and finding harmony with these rhythms helps tremendously as parents because it explains so much of the conflict that comes up with our kids. In order to perform in society, we must demand that both our kids and ourselves go against our natural developmental rhythms, which is irritating and exhausting for everyone. Fortunately, we don't have to go off the grid and move to the wilderness to find harmony or a way to balance our needs. That being said, almost all of us could benefit from sorting out ways to slow down more often.

In this chapter, we look at just a fraction of the biological, psychological, and cognitive processes that continually occur throughout our parenting day. Because we are pulled in so many directions as parents, it helps to look at what's doing the pulling without our awareness. One reason even great parenting programs can somehow translate into another list of shoulds in our day-to-day practice is because they are typically based on a singular comprehensive strategy or on just one scientific theory based in one perspective, be it neuroscience, psychology, or cognition. Each step in Sigh, See, Start addresses the many different internal systems at work in our day—neurological, biological, psychological, cognitive—as well as the external world and all of that which is outside of our control. As a pediatrician, I am used to considering the connections and interplays between multiple branches of science and how to integrate them in simple ways. Sigh, See, Start harnesses insights from a diverse range of scientific viewpoints in order to help us thrive in the complexity and messiness of human relationships. With this greater understanding of the science behind what is happening at each of the three steps in Sigh, See, Start, we will be able to appreciate better why we and our children do what we do; to be more patient; to choose deliberately (rather than only react); and to dare to make individual decisions for our families in any context.

THE SCIENCE OF SIGH

Sometimes when parents begin using Sigh, See, Start, they view the sighing as a placeholder, a reminder to pause before they act. And it certainly is that, but it's so much more. There are a lot of techniques that suggest pausing before you act or methods that recommend deep breathing, but sighing is the most natural because it has such a valuable and specific function in the body. When we sigh, we stimulate the vagus nerve in the parasympathetic nervous system, which initiates a powerful shift in our brains: it can help us move out of stress and upset into a calmer state. In doing so, the vagus nerve brings our higher-level thinking back online, which in turn can communicate to our ancient animal brain to chill; we are safe.

How to sigh properly: Try simply sighing the way you normally would. Or take in a deep breath and release it immediately, letting it out slowly and smoothly. If possible, imagine it's a sigh of contentment or relief. But if you can't do that, at least let your exasperation and frustration out with the breath. I find sighing three times works best when I'm really worked up. Please avoid holding your breath, as you might have learned from other breathing techniques, because this may elevate your heart rate. Instead, simply let the breath go slowly to calm your system down.

Our nervous system is always scanning to see if we are safe. Most parents have heard of the fight, flight, or freeze responses, but they may have no idea how much they affect our daily lives with our kids. These responses come from our autonomic nervous system (ANS), which regulates our body functions. The ANS operates outside of our conscious control; it keeps things running so we don't have to think about them. For instance, it's in charge of resting and digesting after we eat or speeding up our heart rate and breathing if we are exercising. And when it comes to what doctors are taught in medical school, that's about all most of us know about the ANS.

But over the past few decades, neuroscientists have discovered that the autonomic nervous system does a whole lot more than we realized. While there are different theories about how the ANS works, my favorite is the polyvagal theory (PVT) developed by Stephen Porges, a neuroscientist and professor of psychiatry at the University of North Carolina. His PVT makes sense of people's experiences and has been increasingly adopted by pediatric occupational therapists, as well as psychotherapists who work with all ages.

According to Porges's research, our ANS functions as an integrated sensory system that is constantly observing our environment for cues of threat or safety, a process he calls "neuroception." This constant surveillance happens at a preconscious level at the speed of microseconds, so that sometimes we react to things in our environments without even knowing what we're reacting to, or recognizing that we are reacting at all. For example, our nervous systems process low-frequency or deep rumbling noises—such as fireworks, jackhammers, construction noises, and the garbage trucks that upset my dogs—as threatening. In nature, low-frequency noises are rare and almost always signal danger: the low growl of a predator, a thunderstorm, or the sound of an avalanche. Our ANS, which is ancient, recognizes such noises as threats and reacts with the fight-or-flight response, which explains why studies show that people who live in areas with significant noise pollution have higher stress levels and blood pressure, as well as other health issues.[55]

In addition to the environment, the ANS is also constantly scanning other people for signs of safety or threat. Unconsciously, we notice each other's tone of voice, body language, breathing patterns, and all sorts of little cues, like whether a person's facial expression matches what they're saying. Then, our ANS reacts to these cues at a preconscious level, determining whether we are safe or under threat, and we don't get a choice about how we react. That is why, when your kids are having big emotions, you may get sucked into their emotional intensity, despite intellectually understanding that not getting a second lollipop is not a terribly consequential event in their lives, though it is upsetting for them in that moment.

This system is part of why humans sync up with each other, catching each other's moods like they are contagious. It makes good sense when you consider our ancestral environment, when we lived in small familial groups or tribes in direct contact with nature. Back then we needed our group to tell us whether we were safe. And signals of danger needed to be passed very quickly, possibly even without sound, because our group needed to be able to respond immediately and in a coordinated way if we were under attack. So, we evolved to read each other minutely and instantaneously and to react without taking time for the slow process of thought. But what that means for us in our highly complex modern social system is that our nervous system must process overwhelming amounts of social cues and sensory information and then not interpret the information as life or death. We may find ourselves stressed by daily life because, in part, we are living with nervous systems attuned to a slower, unplugged, more physically vulnerable way of life.

The Three States of the ANS

Research on the ANS has long identified three states in all mammals: tend-and-befriend, fight-or-flight, and freeze-or-faint. Porges's polyvagal theory organizes these responses hierarchically based on when they appeared in our evolutionary history, and then uses that to explain when and why these responses show up.

First came the reptiles, who have only one defense when they are under threat: they freeze. Sometimes called "playing dead," the freeze-or-faint response happens when our nervous system decides that the situation is so overwhelming or life-threatening that the best thing to do is to shut down. Think of a rabbit caught in the jaws of a fox, hanging limp and lifeless. In its most extreme form, the shutdown response numbs pain and helps us separate from our bodies in order to make dying easier. Porges locates the freeze response in the dorsal (toward the back) portion of the vagus nerve, which controls the parasympathetic portion of the autonomic nervous system, and calls it the "immobilization" response, which best describes all its functions.

Eventually, ancestral vertebrates developed another defensive response, called the fight-or-flight or "mobilization" response, controlled by the sympathetic nerve. The animal instantaneously gets ready for action: the heart rate goes up, the breathing gets faster and more shallow, energy is redirected from all unnecessary activities like digestion to be used for defense and survival. And whether the animal fights or flees is not under conscious control—the ANS decides preconsciously. The same is true for us as humans.

When warm-blooded animals like mammals evolved from ancient long-extinct reptiles about 200 million years ago, they retained the vagus nerve's freeze-or-faint and gained a new "ventral" vagal pathway that could down-regulate their powerful fight-or-flight mobilization reactions mediated by the sympathetic nervous system. This tend-and-befriend or social response was not for defense, but for times of safety. So, like our beloved dogs, if humans are getting cues of safety from our environment and we're with people we think we can trust, then we are likely to manifest our social nervous system. When that happens, branches of the ventral vagus nerve that connect to our faces and vocal cords activate. Our faces become open, our eyes are expressive, and our voices become more musical with an up-and-down pattern to our speech called prosody. The social engagement system allows us to be excited and playful or calm and soothing and continues to send messages of safety to others around us who are picking up on our cues. These biobehavioral signals of safety (or distress) have a profound effect on others, something that becomes obvious when we consider the way a mother responds to her infant's crying, calming her infant with a soothing, singsong voice.

But the moment we detect a threat such as a low-frequency noise, a sharp tone of voice, or an angry look, the sympathetic nerve starts to take over. (And when we consider that this happens many times over the course of a day, it is truly remarkable how much "threat" and regulation our nervous systems are processing.) As fight-or-flight comes online, our heart rate and blood pressure go up, stress hormones release into our blood streams, our muscles grow tense, and our voices and facial expressions become flatter. And all of this is transmitted to everyone around us lightning fast so that they can enter a state of defense and readiness for danger immediately, whether they recognize what just happened to them or not.

From a psychological perspective, we experience fight-or-flight as anxiety, which can be triggered by a "threat" as simple as feeling overwhelmed. And because sympathetic activation shuts down the parts of our brains responsible for higher-level thinking, which is deemed as a waste of energy in this survival state, we (just like our kids) cannot and do not respond reasonably when we are in fight-or-flight.

If we feel so overwhelmed that our nervous system decides we can't fight or flee, the ANS triggers the shutdown and immobilization response of freeze or feint. Emotionally, this feels like depression, and sometimes even dissociation. If you've ever felt that heavy feeling like you just want to sleep or give up when faced with too much, you know what the shutdown response feels like. It also protects us from emotional threats, because we disengage from social interaction.

Ideally, a functioning nervous system has access to all three of these responses when we need them. We can flexibly and relatively easily move between the states, depending on what we need at the time.

So, what does all of this mean? It means that we need active tools throughout the day to help us respond to threats—information or signals that our nervous system reads as dangerous, but that are innocuous in our modern life, like flashing lights in a store window.

There are many ways to signal to ourselves that we are not under threat, and sighing is one of the easiest. You can do it anywhere, at any time. When we sigh, we tell our own nervous systems that we are safe by simulating the behaviors of the social tend-and-befriend state. If we bring our voices into our chests and add expression and more musical tone, or if we relax our facial expression and smile, we often find we start to feel different. Deep pressure is also a great way to stimulate the vagus nerve, so try pressing on your thighs with your hands or squeezing the fleshy part of your hand. Regulating ourselves can't be rushed. It takes the time it takes because safety feels unrushed. But when we do something like sighing, the simple action of breathing out slowly tells our nervous system that we are safe because it is so different from the way we breathe when we are in danger. If we run or fight we breathe fast, and if we are hiding we may hold our breath. But we only sigh when we are safe.[56]

However, sometimes you may find that your sighing is not calming you down at all, because in addition to all of the external stimuli that may be activating your alarm system, there are internal physiological processes at work, too. Often without our awareness, we may be acting out patterned behavior that we learned as a child. For example, we may experience the feeling of being disrespected as a kind of threat, because for most of human history our social status has been directly tied to our ability to keep ourselves safe. When sighing won't snap you out of it, taking time to bring your awareness to what you are thinking and feeling in the moment while continuing to sigh may. It's not helpful to try to hold every influence on your behavior in conscious awareness all the time—that will just drive you crazy. But bringing our awareness to one or two threads from time to time has—in my experience, both as a parent who practices Sigh, See, Start and as someone who coaches people in it—brought enormous awareness, calm, and clarity.

When we sigh, we not only offer ourselves a chance to calm down, but we allow for something even more powerful: an ability to connect with our own bodies and become present in the way our kids need us to be. In fact, a great deal of our children's annoying behavior is motivated by trying to get our full attention, to get us to be present with them, rather than distracted by the rush and worry of life.

THE SCIENCE OF SEE

After we've sighed to tend to our own need for safety and to connect with our bodies, we are often in a calmer and more self-aware state. In this new place, we give ourselves a chance to be fully present for our next step. We have an opportunity to observe our child as they are, with an understanding that we are capable and we can figure out a way forward—even if we don't yet know what that way is!

The Stories We Tell Ourselves

To function in our daily lives, we assume that our perception of the world is accurate. We are blissfully unaware of all the information that we don't notice. Cognitive scientists now believe that the key function of the human brain is "meaning-making." Our brains take in extraordinary amounts of information, both from within our own bodies and from our external environments, each microsecond; the brain then sorts which information is important and which is not. The input that makes the cut is either handled unconsciously by our brain, or it is forwarded up to our consciousness. As one science writer puts it, "Brains sample information, hold it briefly, construct meaning, and then discard the information."[57]

Our conscious mind is entirely unaware of this process, and thus we believe we have complete information about the item at which we are looking. But in actuality, we are looking at an interpretation of preselected information that our brain has served up to us, only after filtering the raw data through our beliefs, preconceived ideas, and so on. We are never consciously aware of the information our brains have discarded, and, so, we don't know what we don't know. That may seem like a problem until we consider that in its unfiltered state, even the small amount of information that makes it to our consciousness would feel like overwhelming chaos. Our brains prevent that overload by organizing the information into systems of meaning. These systems have been formed by our cultural heritage, education, and life experience. That's why when I see a funny shadow in the corner of my eye, I perceive it as a feature of an energy form called light. But my Celtic ancestors might have perceived the same shadow as a creature of the faerie folk moving between worlds. Both perceptions would have been produced by the same rational meaning-making process, and both of us would have been sure of the reality of our conclusions.

If the way our brains handle information seems wild, consider the way we make decisions. Moran Cerf, a former computer hacker once hired by a bank to rob it as a security test, is now a neuroscientist and business school professor at Northwestern University who studies how we make decisions. His lab has run numerous studies on decision-making, some of which include results drawn from accessing the brain directly by putting electrodes on the exposed neurons of volunteers undergoing brain surgery. The findings are shocking. Instead of making the conscious, rational, and deliberate decisions we think we make, our brains assess risk, make choices about how to keep us safe, and do it all before we are cognitively aware of these assessments and choices. After we make a decision, our brains create a story to explain why we made the choice we made. Only the last part, the story we create, makes it to our consciousness.[58]

If the decision is particularly important, then aspects of our personalities also get involved, and where we fall on the "big five" personality traits can "govern a lot of the mechanisms we use to make decisions and 'see the world.'"[59] The big five—openness, conscientiousness, extraversion, agreeableness, neuroticism—are the key traits of personality that scientists study, and there are many free quizzes available online for those who wish to learn more about their own personalities. But here's one example of how a personality trait could impact decision-making as a parent. Let's say your child asks you to go to a water park with a friend. If you are high in extraversion and openness (curious and willing to try new things), you may easily say yes, reasoning that it will be fun and a good experience for your child. After all, they've had swimming lessons, the parent who is taking them seems responsible, and there are lifeguards at the park. On the other hand, if you are high in conscientiousness (you prefer schedules and pay attention to details) and neuroticism (you are prone to worry), you may say no, or insist that you join the excursion. After all, you don't want your child to miss out on fun, but you've read about kids drowning at those places, and you prefer to keep your own eyes on your child when they are in the water (as many drowning-prevention experts recommend). While the other parent seems fine, you've never seen them drive, and the park is forty-five minutes away. It would be safer to drive the kids yourself.[60]

One particularly interesting part of the way our brains make meaning out of raw information has to do with how they deal with missing information. Brains insert what they expect when they don't have all the information. And that can cause big problems in human relationships, because we tend to decide what's going on in other people's heads without even knowing we are doing it.

As parents, simply knowing that our opinion on what's going on with our kids or what their motives are is a story we tell ourselves can change a lot. And it certainly gives a new perspective on our kids' behavior when we consider that they, too, are reacting to us based on the stories their brains are telling them. Practicing mindful seeing—the see step in Sigh, See, Start—is a quick way to get in the habit of letting go of our stories in order to learn what's actually going on with our kids.

Seeing Mindfully

To see is to practice mindfulness, a practice so hyped in the last decade that our reaction might be something like "ugh, not this again." Bear with me. Try for a moment to forget everything you've heard about mindfulness so we can look at it simply and from the viewpoint of how it can help us as parents.

Mindfulness means that we observe the present moment, both within us (as we did during sigh) and outside of us (as we may do during see), and we accept what we find without trying to criticize or change it (at least, not just yet.) We are being self-scientists. We observe what it is that we are working with, trusting that we will be able to handle it. Mindfulness researcher Mark Williams explains it this way: "When unhappiness or stress hovers overhead, rather than taking it personally, you learn to treat them as if they were black clouds in the sky, and to observe them with friendly curiosity as they drift past."[61] Mindful awareness takes notice of our thoughts, moods, or the states of our ANS; it moves them out of our blind spots and into our awareness, so we can then choose how to behave or react.

Mindfulness, then, is a lot less time-consuming than we've all been led to believe. In previous chapters, we saw many examples of parents who used the see step successfully without having a meditation or yoga practice. Sighing to be with ourselves and seeing the situation as it is are the essence of mindfulness, and they can take very little time. The aim is to let go of the resistance or avoidance patterns many of us rely upon and to let things be what they are (uncomfortable thoughts, feelings, and behaviors within us or our children that we might normally judge as unacceptable). This is information we desperately need to parent wisely.

Mindful parenting is a big topic for researchers, who consistently find the practice yields benefits for both parents and kids. Parents report less stress, better emotional health, more affection for their kids, and more pleasure in parenting. Meanwhile, kids show greater wellbeing and self-regulation, as well as fewer behavior problems or instances of substance abuse in adolescence. The connection between mindfulness and achieving the outcomes every parent wants is not obvious, until you consider the behaviors mindfulness brings out in parents. Mindful parents show emotional awareness, nonjudgmental acceptance of, and compassion for self and child. They engage in listening with full attention and regulate themselves in parent-child interactions.[62]

However, one recent study found that most people use mindfulness incorrectly, and then miss out on the benefits. Because of words like *nonjudgement* or *acceptance*, a lot of people interpret mindfulness as passively letting what happens happen, which is not mindfulness at all. Rather, mindful acceptance involves a profound engagement with a problem and all its attendant negative emotions. True mindfulness is a lot more than simply becoming fully aware of a stressor: it means grappling with that stressor, without avoiding it or going for a short cut. Mindfulness is hard work.[63]

Sigh, See, Start gives parents a way to use mindfulness in the moment, requires no additional training, and helps us move between states in our ANS and to show up as calm, curious, wise parents. Because using the method in real time integrates mindfulness into our lives, it is not even necessary to take up a traditional mindfulness practice like meditation or yoga. Micro-moments of mindfulness like those we get with Sigh, See, Start may actually have a greater benefit than meditating.

When psychotherapist and mindfulness teacher Jake Eagle taught a course called "Thrilled to Be Alive," something remarkable happened. Eagle had discovered that about half the students in his course were not doing the ten-minute daily meditations due to lack of time. So, he suggested that instead they meditate for a few seconds at a time. The surprise came when at the end of the course, the students who were "micro-meditating" reported equal or better benefits than the students doing longer meditations.[64] And this makes a lot of sense. The purpose of mindfulness meditation is to change the way we live in the moment-to-moment rush of our lives. Making that kind of change requires us to integrate what begins as a separate activity. On the other hand, Sigh, See, Start teaches us momentary mindfulness in our parenting lives right from the beginning, so it's no surprise that parents get results quickly.

Some parents are initially hesitant to try mindfulness because they worry it conflicts with their religious beliefs. So, it helps to know that historically, practically every religion has its own version of a mindfulness practice. Christians are taught to be aware of their inner motives as they seek to express love and mercy, and until recently had a widespread and robust monastic practice of mindful contemplation. The Jewish and Muslim traditions have their own practices of spiritual meditation. Hinduism has a long tradition of yogic meditation and asanas, while Buddhism is the best known for mindful meditation and is often credited as the origin of our current secular practices. Meanwhile, Confucian meditation involves disciplined attention to one's situation and mental phenomena.[65] Prayer in general has long been used as a form of meditation. For example, those who practice Santería may use songs to the orisha in this way.[66] Further, researchers have noted that today's mindfulness practices have parallels to the ancient and ongoing practices of many Indigenous people, the world over.[67] Jeanne Corrigal, a spiritual teacher in the Canadian Métis community, says, "When I first encountered mindfulness, I thought, 'This is our teaching, our Indigenous teaching of how to be in the world, how to be in connection with the world.'"[68]

A word of warning: mindfulness practice, like any medical treatment, can have side effects, which are rarely talked about. By coming fully into the present moment and letting ourselves become aware of everything, we risk sensory overload. That is exactly what happens to some people: they become more irritable when using mindfulness, while still handling stress better overall.[69] Since I am not aware of a research study that addresses how to manage this, I'll share my personal opinion: Mindfulness is great, in balance, but not to the point that we are so much in the present moment that we stop using all of our other fabulous talents as humans, such as our ability to disconnect from an irritating present and daydream about the future. Both are needed; both are valuable. For myself, as a person who already tends toward sensory sensitivity, I find that Sigh, See, Start is often the right amount of mindfulness for me. In my experience, the micro-moments of mindfulness I get with Sigh, See, Start bring just the right amount of awareness and connection, without irritating me.

THE SCIENCE OF START

When parents face getting started, they commonly hesitate, worried that they could get it wrong or mess it up. In this section we'll look at why there is no need to worry about getting it exactly right because it is in the process of trying that we learn what works and what doesn't. When we allow ourselves to gravitate naturally toward our strengths in parenting, positive changes begin to occur. Plus, researchers are uncovering what many of us may have intuited: that our love is what matters most with regard to how kids turn out. Start trusting that your love for your kids is what matters most.

As a mom, I have all the same worries that other parents do. Most of all, I worry that I will not be enough and that I will fail my kids in a way that harms them in the future. That's why I tell myself as often as I tell the parents I see in my pediatric office that the number one determinant of whether a kid ends up okay is our love. That's it. It's not our perfect parenting technique or whether we gave them the right opportunities—it's simply that they feel our affection.

In 2016, Harvard University founded the Human Flourishing Program with a mission to study and promote human flourishing, a concept the program's director, Tyler VanderWeele, describes as "a state in which all aspects of a person's life are good." Flourishing covers five domains of life: happiness and life satisfaction, physical and mental health, meaning and purpose, good character, and good relationships in the social dimension. In other words, a flourishing life is the kind of robustly satisfying life we all want for our kids.

When VanderWeele and his team set out to study how experiences in childhood impact whether we flourish in adulthood, they found that the only factor that seemed to matter consistently was whether people experienced their parents as warm and loving when they were kids. If adults had warm, affectionate parents, they were particularly likely to have a sense of purpose in life, and they also were happier, had better social lives, and were less likely to suffer from depression, anxiety, or drug use.[70]

Initially, I had my doubts. Could love really be enough? What about how well parents provide structure or enrichment or any of the other things pediatricians worry about? Fortunately, a few months later VanderWeele reached out with his team's next study, which evaluated both whether adults recalled their parents as warm and loving and what parenting style their parents used. When researchers look at parenting style, they ask both how demanding of and how responsive to their children parents were. When we leave out parents who engage in a pattern of abuse or neglect (which do not leave a child feeling loved), the three main parenting styles have been described as the authoritative, the authoritarian, and the permissive styles.

Research consistently shows that between authoritative, authoritarian, and permissive parenting styles, authoritative is the best for kids. Such parents show high levels of love and boundary setting. They have high (but fair) expectations of their children and they are very engaged with them. They show high levels of nurturing, involvement, and sensitivity while encouraging autonomy and reasoning in children.

In contrast, authoritarian parents demand everything and show little affection. They show highly directive behaviors, high levels of restriction, and power-asserting behaviors. It's what I often refer to as old-school: the message the child gets is "Do what I say. What you want, your need for independence, and your feelings are not important." However, it's important to acknowledge that in the days of old-school parenting many parents applied it in an authoritarian, controlling way, while others were more authoritative and showed a great deal of affection.

On the other end of the spectrum are the permissive parents, who just want their kids to be happy. This was a style that came into vogue in the 1990s. Such parents demand and expect very little of their children, but they are highly responsive to their children's needs and feelings. Their behavior is noncontrolling, and they use little punishment. They rely on being warm and loving with their kids.

In the past, research has shown that both authoritarian and permissive parenting styles have more negative outcomes for children, so VanderWeele's team expected their study would have the same results. When it came to controlling, authoritarian parents, the study found what others had: offspring had more depression and lower flourishing in adulthood. But when they looked at permissive parents, the research team was surprised. Instead of reinforcing the previous research findings that permissive parenting led to higher risk of mental illness in offspring, this study found only a weak association between the two. The research team thought this had to do with the way they looked at the data ("this study considered parenting styles as continuous variables"[71]) while prior studies used either/or definitions. So, if the parents were extremely permissive, it wasn't great for the kids. But if they were more generally permissive, their children's experience of feeling loved as a child was protective later in adulthood. In other words, when people felt loved, other aspects of their parents' styles mattered a lot less.

Nevertheless, VanderWeele's team did confirm that the kids who did the best in adulthood were the ones with authoritative parents, who provided rules and discipline and showed lots of love. Specifically, greater parental authoritativeness was associated with greater emotional processing and emotional expression, fewer depressive symptoms, and lower risk of overeating in adult offspring (when comparing the top 33 percent to the bottom 33 percent).

It's worth noting that because this study looked at the effect of parenting styles on adults, it did not specifically study the recent epidemic of invasive overparenting, which we discussed in Part 1. Other researchers have found overparenting has a clear negative impact on kids. Sigh, See, Start can help parents who realize they've been overparenting break those habits.

When I asked VanderWeele what he thought about these results, he told me, "I do not think that the results indicate that rules and discipline are irrelevant for children.... What the results do make clear, though, is that love or warmth is the dominant element." He went on to tell me how he and his wife, like all parents, debate their decisions about parenting. After this study, while those decisions still matter to him, he finds, "It is also good to know, at the end of the day, that simply trying to love our children well will go a long way." He takes comfort in the thought that parents have a powerful effect when they love their children and do their best for them.[72]

Knowing that showing our kids affection and love is the bottom line can bring us tremendous peace as parents. And Sigh, See, Start harnesses the confidence that loving our kids and doing the best we can for their welfare is what matters most by helping us practice bringing ourselves to our kids, instead of a technique.

Start Using Your Strengths

Parents who use Sigh, See, Start consistently talk about how much more confident they feel. Instead of trying to fix your flaws as a parent, Sigh, See, Start teaches you to start valuing your own abilities as a parent. This is an inherently strengths-based perspective, because I believe that you already have the strengths you need to parent well—you just need practice using them instead of letting the shoulds run the show.

As a pediatrician, I know that your child, no matter how young they are or how many special needs they have, also has their own developing strengths that they can use. The more you observe your child, the more you will see their strengths, and the more you will learn to work with them.

When using Sigh, See, Start, the only way you can avoid growing confident in your own and your child's strengths is if you let the ShouldStorm hijack the way you practice Sigh, See, Start, trying to turn it into a way to "make your child behave" or to "fix" yourself or your child into what they "should" be. The method does not work that way, but that doesn't mean we won't each misuse Sigh, See, Start at least once before we realize this.

Pediatricians and those who study child development have long held the strengths-based perspective. So much of the behavior of developing children has to do with kids experimenting with their emerging talents. That means that much of what parents find annoying or unacceptable in their child is actually related to that child's natural strengths and temperament. For instance, a stubborn, persistent child who "wants their own way" will often grow into an adult we admire for their grit and stick-to-it-iveness. The very personality trait that was a "flaw" in the three-year-old is highly praised in the fifty-five-year-old business leader. So rather than teaching that child to feel ashamed of their defiance, we can raise them with love and appropriate limits, so that one day they can use their persistence as part of a thriving life.

The term "strengths-based" also refers to a specific model of psychology first advanced by Donald Clifton and his research with the Gallup organization. He began studying highly successful people and found out that they did things very differently from the majority. Instead of working on improving their weaknesses, as we are all taught to do by our culture and our schools, they focused on playing to their strengths. If they were bad at something, they didn't waste time and effort trying to get good at it. Instead, they found someone else who was good at it to work with.[73] Clifton's project with Gallup has collected over fifty years' worth of robust data on successful people's strengths, and uses that data to help both adults and kids to identify some of their own strengths in order to develop them.

In the book *Strengths Based Parenting*, psychologist Mary Reckmeyer applies the Clifton model to parenting. Because a large body of research shows that people are happier and do a better job when they are using their strengths and doing what they are good at, Reckmeyer believes we can parent with a lot more happiness and a lot less stress if we identify our strengths. "Every parent and every child is unique," she writes, "There is no one right way to bring up a child. There is only the way you do it, given your talents, strengths, and environment."[74]

Perhaps you are like me: full of creative ideas for your kids' play, but not so good at organizing, and your playroom and kids' rooms are so messy with toys, books, Legos, dress-up costumes, and art supplies that you can't find anything. Instead of wasting time and energy trying to correct your weakness, the strengths-based model would suggest you bring in someone who already has that strength. Maybe your friend who just loves organizing could do a walk-through and give you ideas about what types of bins to buy and how to set things up. Or maybe you could binge-watch a home organization show: that's what I did, and it took our home from total chaos to controlled chaos. And because I've learned that it's okay for me to play to my strengths as a parent, I'm going to accept that my kids are not going to grow up with a perfectly tidy or organized home.

When Rebekah's kids took the talent questionnaire from *Strengths Based Parenting*, she was amazed. "I felt so relieved because my son's behavior finally made sense," she said. He came up with a talent for "competing," which according to the book meant that he saw every day as a game to play and was driven to win. Because he was full of self-motivation that often helped to motivate others, winning would bring him satisfaction and happiness, but losing would feel intensely bad, and could lead kids like him to get angry or even to cry.[75] "This makes so much sense," Rebekah observed. "He is so driven about his interests, but he can be so playful and funny."

Lately, as Rebekah's son had hit adolescence, he was picking on his younger siblings more, commenting on their weaknesses and always trying to one-up them. Meanwhile, his younger sibling's strengths test had revealed a talent for "presence," a natural ability to command attention and to easily capture the interest of others.[76] "Now I know why my older son has been so annoyed when his brother takes center stage—it's a competition he's not winning," Rebekah explained. She reasoned that his recent efforts to take his brother down were really about trying to find a way to win.

"We need to be careful about how we judge kids," writes Reckmeyer. "We can make them doubt themselves…. We can even crush them. But we can't really change them. We can't make them who they aren't, but we can make it easier and happier for them to be who they are."[77] That's exactly how Rebekah used her newfound insights into her son. By seeing his behavior through the lens of emerging strengths, Rebekah felt she could now start coaching her son through his intensely competitive feelings and give him some ideas on how to compete more effectively. She thought one of her son's other talents could be helpful here. He'd also come up with "discovering," the desire to learn and become an expert on subjects that mattered to him. "Maybe I can get him interested in learning how his sense of fun and humor is a way to get some of the attention his brother gets without turning other people off by being unkind. It's a better way to win," said Rebekah.

The experience of understanding her son's unwelcome behavior through the lens of a frustrated strength also brought some healing to Rebekah herself. "I'm sure I would have gotten 'competing' if I had taken this test as a kid. I feel like now I can forgive my younger self for always wanting to win and being an ugly winner, not to mention a sore loser. I really understand my son because I remember how bad I felt when I didn't win." She was excited to look for some new activities to encourage her son's talent for competing.

This strengths-based approach is the exact opposite of the dominant viewpoint in our culture, as in one Gallup survey that found that 52 percent of Americans think that knowing your strengths and developing them is less helpful to life success than knowing your weaknesses and working on them. In contrast, Reckmeyer shares the story of Roy Spence, who frequently got poor grades on his school papers due to spelling errors. One day his mother told him, "Son, you can't spell, but you can write." She told him to do his best in school, but when it came to his life, "I do not want you to waste any of your precious time or talent trying to be average at what you are bad at. I want you to spend your life becoming great at what you are good at." Later, Roy founded a successful marketing and communications company and authored several books.[78]

I think every parent should tell their kids what Roy's mom told him. But as a pediatrician, I can't help but clarify that a strengths-based perspective does not mean ignoring true developmental delays. When a child who can't spell gets diagnosed with dyslexia, it's worth getting them an Orton-Gillingham or Wilson tutor, who can teach them to read and write successfully through a proven method specially designed for kids with dyslexia. The goal is to support them so that the learning difficulty doesn't get in the way of using their talents. We're not trying to make them a national spelling-bee champion. We're not even going for As on spelling tests. We are lightening the burden just enough that they can go after their strengths. "Children learn and grow better when they put their energy toward what they *can* do rather than slaving away on what they struggle with," writes Reckmeyer.[79]

Sigh, See, Start Is the Process of Science

Science is not, as so many of us learned in school, the truth—a set of correct and true facts. Rather, science is a way to keep discovering more of what the truth might be, limited only by what questions we ask, who or what we study, or the limits of our technology.

Unfortunately, medical and psychological science carry an ugly past history of prejudices against women, minority groups, and even children, who were once considered unimportant to study or actively targeted, such as by the study of eugenics. But the process of science itself, when practiced ethically, is one of the finest tools we humans have ever created.

What we "know," based on gradual, messy scientific discovery, is always changing because we are always learning more. Science represents much of the best of what it means to be human: curiosity, wonder, tinkering, innovating, the desire to cure or heal, change, and hope. It's a process based on the premise that we can figure things out, and I don't know a better foundation for confidence in life than that.

In a similar way, Sigh, See, Start is the embodiment of the belief that we, as parents, can figure things out. In fact, as a process, Sigh, See, Start *is* science: it's a personalized version of the scientific method. We sigh to become aware of our emotions, assumptions, and shoulds so we can release them in order to see clear-eyed observations. Then we start generating a hypothesis about what might work, testing it, and adapting what we do based on the results of our experiments. The more we run the cycle, the more we learn and the more success we have, and the more fun we have engaging our curiosity. And the more we learn about ourselves and our kids, the more satisfied we all feel as our kids' trust in our ability to understand them and connect with them grows.

The process of constantly observing and learning like this comes with a challenge: we have to get used to feeling uncertain. Asking questions and leaning into uncertainty may be how we grow, but it's also uncomfortable. In fact, it's that very discomfort that the Should-Storm offers to solve for us; sometimes being bullied by criticism feels better than uncertainty.

It may be hard work to learn how to question our interpretations and decisions or to practice leaning into the uncertainty that constantly updating our old beliefs with new knowledge brings, but it's the only way I know for parents to keep up with the wonderful and complicated way our kids are constantly growing, adapting, and revealing new parts of themselves as they grow. And fortunately, Sigh, See, Start makes that process a whole lot easier and builds parents' confidence in their ability to manage a little uncertainty much faster than I had ever expected. I think it's because we are motivated by our deep love for our kids.

CHAPTER 5 : KEY TAKEAWAYS

....

- You already have everything you need to be a wonderful parent.
- Our nervous system is always scanning for threats and then syncs up with the nervous systems of those nearby.
- The ANS has three states: social and connected, fight or flight/mobilized, and freeze or feint/immobilized.
- Sighing helps us regulate our nervous system to help us feel safe.
- Our brains are wired to create meaning, even when it doesn't have all the information. This means our perceptions of our children are often stories we tell ourselves and can be wrong.
- The See step is a quick way to let go of our stories to find out what is really going on with our kids.
- The most important factor for a child's future is whether they experience their parents as warm and loving.
- Understand and use your strengths as a parent, rather than trying to fix your weaknesses.
- Using Sigh, See, Start is a personalized version of the scientific method. By clarifying our assumptions, testing our ideas, and then adapting to the results of our experiments, our wisdom as parents grows rapidly.

PART 3

LIVING AND PARENTING WITH A SIGH, SEE, START MINDSET

Chapter 6

Raising the Family You Have

Don't let what you cannot do interfere with what you can do.
—John Wooden, basketball coach

L eaving an unhealthy culture like our parenting ShouldStorm happens in stages and over time. The first stage is naming and understanding the culture, as we did in Part 1 of this book—becoming aware of its belief system, and how it drives us to parent burnout. The next stage is learning how to approach experiences in new and graceful ways, such as we did in Part 2, when we examined the Sigh, See, Start method. However, as long as we simply stand in opposition to the high-pressure parenting culture, we are still in the culture. We are still using a perfectionist mindset as our standard, and then reacting to it and resisting it. Until we replace the ShouldStorm with something new, we will keep slipping back into the same old patterns. We need a healthy, internalized belief system about ourselves and our kids.

The third stage is, thus, the process of self-discovery and changing our parenting mindset to one of strength, confidence, and presence.

That sounds like a lot, I know. But, through the continued practice of Sigh, See, Start, we begin to see our strengths, our parenting abilities, our children's inherent worth, and our family in its beautiful imperfection; we bring ourselves into the moment. We respect and support ourselves in difficult parenting situations, make connections with our children, and give the whole family the grace to make mistakes and figure out how to proceed. And in doing all of this, we start to raise the family we have. Not the family we wish we had, or the family we've been told we should have, but the one we actually have.

A Sigh, See, Start Mindset

As a younger pediatrician, I was frequently puzzled by the way parents focused so much on keeping their kids comfortable physically and emotionally to the point of coddling them while the kids were young, and then suddenly shifted to become pushy parents as the kids advanced in school. The same parents who would interrupt our medical visits for the slightest whimper from their four-year-old now seemed almost callously indifferent to that same child's anxiety and burnout about school or competitive sports as an eleven-year-old. However, when my own kids got to middle school, I understood. Like the parents in my practice, I was driven by anxiety and insecurity about not doing enough to help my kids succeed in this competitive and harsh world.

When I began to research the chaotic and shaming parenting culture that we live in, I started to formulate and then practice Sigh, See, Start. From there, I noticed that it wasn't just the practice of Sigh, See, Start that made a difference in how I parented, but that the practice and the results I was seeing created a whole new self-view. I began to see—and seeing is believing—that I was a good parent. I was not perfect and I made mistakes, but I got us through a lot of hard and wonderful things.

With an ever-growing belief that I was enough and could handle proactive parenting, Sigh, See, Start prompted me to become present and mindful of the current situation and then ask, "What do I do now?" Through continued practice of being present with your child, or moving yourself into a regulated state, you will show yourself that you are more than enough. You will help your child through something really hard, model self-respect, and see that you are capable. If you show up in a regulated, present way just one time more this week than you did the week before, you have automatically reduced the gap between what you think you should be and what your child actually needs from you.

Presence

In previous chapters I discussed the concept of mindful acceptance: that we accept the reality in front of us. Buddhist and mindfulness practices have been expressed for centuries in languages other than English; when we try to translate concepts rich with meaning from one language to another, the words we choose are approximate, as is the case with *acceptance*. In English, the word *acceptance* becomes problematic, because it implies that we are passively embracing something, which loses the sense of active engagement that the concept had in the original languages. I find that the English word *presence* works better. To be mindfully present means that you do not fight the issue, nor do you have to love it, but you are being with it, as it is. It implies a pause in action and reaction, being mindful, paying attention to things as they are—and staying with ourselves in this moment, too. When we move into action, when we start, we bring that same presence to what we do, basing our decisions on the present reality.

* * *

On the morning of January 13, 2022, I tested positive for COVID-19, and by that evening I was desperately ill. I struggled to breathe for months. Eventually I was diagnosed with long COVID, an illness that has impacted most of my body systems. Over a year later, I must spend at least three hours each day in bed. I have memory and concentration problems often called "brain fog," and I spend days at a time looking like I have a combination of influenza, the stomach flu, and encephalitis, with super-weird neurological symptoms every week or two. My husband has had to pick up all the slack, as I can no longer run errands, walk the dogs, or do household chores.

Before long COVID, I was "that mom"; my friends were constantly asking me how I did it all. I was tired, of course, like everyone else I knew, but I was living out my passion. But the day I caught COVID, literally overnight, I went from a full-time practicing pediatrician, speaker, and writer for national publications to a largely homebound disabled person.

As a parent, I have worried tremendously. Was I going to be able to be the parent my children needed? Would I be able to give them enough support to navigate middle school successfully? I couldn't get out of bed or help them with their homework. I had no idea how to parent in this new condition.

But I used Sigh, See, Start. When you are confused and at wit's end, Sigh, See, Start is a place to begin. Even though I lacked the brainpower for just about everything, I realized that I was able to be present with my children, and that that went a long, long way for them during this difficult time. For instance, after school when one of my sons came into my room, where I was lying in bed, he'd ask me if he could tell me something, and then regale me with some entertaining story about a friend and hand sanitizer. And during these small moments, I was able to give him my full, loving presence. We laughed together a lot. With Sigh, See, Start, I have been able to calm down when I can't breathe or I'm in pain; I have been able to ground myself when my anxiety escalates and I worry about all that I am not able to do. My mindful presence during this time created deep connections for me and my boys, which became a source of strength for us during this difficult period.

I've often observed that much of child or adolescent "misbehavior" is not really misbehavior but the child's effort to get us to be present with them. When we learn to be present as part of a way of living, our kids tend to settle down and decrease the chaos, because they know we are there with them, and that we will be predictably present with them on a regular basis.

Energy Envelope

In learning to live with long COVID, I have had to learn how to pace my life differently. In my pre-COVID life, I packed my waking hours full to the brim with activity and achievement. And I got it all done. Whether it was my years as an athlete, or as a high-achieving student who got through college, medical school, and residency training because of my ability to push through fatigue and keep on going, pushing through had always worked for me. It was not just how I approached school or my work as a pediatrician—it was how I approached hard times or grief in my personal life. But even while I was healthy, this constant pushing was coming at an ever-increasing cost emotionally.

When I developed long COVID, the occupational therapist my doctor referred me to helped me learn about pacing, about tracking my energy and learning to limit my activity to what fit within my energy envelope. It was essential, because if I went beyond that envelope, my symptoms would flare and I would become very ill. But with all that time in bed, I began to reflect on the way I'd been living while I was healthy. Maybe I had an energy envelope then, too. Sure, it was a much bigger one and it had more give, but hadn't there been consequences when I pushed myself too hard? Didn't I become tired and cranky like we all do? It made me wonder about the fast-paced lives we live as modern parents. If you are healthy, you can keep pushing. But should you?

The concept of an energy envelope comes from the observation that people with certain chronic illnesses have better health outcomes and quality of life when they maintain their expended energy at a level consistent with their available energy. Those who over-expend their energy get sicker, while those who stay in their energy envelopes notice some modest improvements.[80]

For a healthy person, exercising a bit past their max can help build capacity, but if they push too far they can get injured. In our hustle culture that advises us to push hard at school and work all the time, we are constantly pushing past our energy envelopes. The result is anxiety, depression, burnout, unhealthy weight gain, and so on.

Learning to pace my activity to match my energy levels and not push beyond them feels like a lesson I should have learned long ago. Now that I might have only thirty productive minutes in a whole day, I had to prioritize what was most important. That meant not giving up all hope and staying in bed all day and not ignoring my limits and pushing beyond what I could do. It meant that I had thirty minutes. What could I do with those minutes? What had to wait? It was hard to decide that some days all I would do was attend a doctor's visit or fill out an insurance form, while other days I might spend that time on writing this book or on having a conversation with my kids or my husband. On days when I got frustrated, and I pushed, I got punished worse than I ever could have imagined — often with severe physical symptoms and an inability to think clearly for days. That natural consequence didn't care about my shoulds — I should be able to do more, I should be able to take care of my kids, and I should be able to do my work.

Sometimes, oftentimes, life's demands do not let up, and we must keep pushing even if we are functioning beyond our energy envelopes. Maybe we need a second job to make ends meet, we are caring for a sick loved one or a child with special needs, we are struggling with our own health, or we are carrying the heavy load of grief or of experiencing injustice or bias against us. We don't always have the choices we need in our lives, but when we do, we are wise if we consider how our energy is used.

What might functioning within your energy envelope look like? Can you do all that you do in a less ambitious timeframe? Can you do things less frequently or for half the time? This is easier said than done, but it can be done. One thing is certain: I learned that my main criteria for evaluating how well I budgeted my energy came down to whether I was able to be mindfully present with my children, even if it was for a short time. If we are too tired or irritable to be lovingly present, then something's got to give.

Raising Kids

You've probably heard that the use of *parent* as a verb was invented relatively recently, in the past several decades. Before we started to parent our kids, people raised their kids. The word *raise* comes from farming and animal husbandry and has traditionally implied that the animal is going to grow up just fine as long as you supply its basic needs. Raising a child suggests that you are bringing up someone with inherent strengths and abilities. They will have limitations and problems, but your job is not to make them different from who or what they are; it is to help them be the best versions of themselves, in this time, and in this society. Parenting, by contrast, has become shorthand for the intensive child cultivation we practice now; it implies the active role parents should play in order to make their children into versions of an ideal that may or may not actually be something you want for your family.

When I was a kid, my mother made a couple of trips a week to the fruit farm just up the mountain from our house. At the time, the commercial supermarkets were full of the extensively bred produce that was considered appealing to consumers: large, perfectly shaped, blemish-free tomatoes and apples. And they were also dull and flavorless and depleted of nutrients. But at the farm, where they grew older breeds of McIntosh apples and New Jersey sweet tomatoes the way it had been done for ages, the produce was small, imperfectly shaped, sometimes marked by a blemish or two, and bursting with flavor. Of course, these days even the commercial supermarkets are bringing in heirloom tomatoes and "ugly fruit," because we now recognize that imperfect produce tastes better and is more nutritious.

Unfortunately, we don't seem to have figured this out with our kids yet, because we are still optimizing, molding, cultivating, enhancing, and over-nurturing them and generally trying to create the ideal child. But just as the overdeveloped tomatoes in the supermarket ended up depleted of nutrition and flavor, modern parenting is pushing our kids to fit an ideal, without developing the substance and resilience they need, and robbing them of the opportunities to develop the interesting personalities childhood used to provide. We end up leaving them to address these developmental tasks in adulthood, when they were meant to be accomplished in childhood.

As Frank Anderson, a psychiatrist and psychologist who specializes in trauma, told me, "I think if you stay out of kids' way, they'll do great."[81] Sigh, See, Start gets us in the habit of stepping back to make room for our kids' strengths and individuality, so that we can try raising them and supporting them on their way. And because Sigh, See, Start trains us to approach all of this process as learning, our kids have space to make lots of mistakes and grow up to be a little imperfect, but full of flavor and substance.

Raising the Kids You Have
(Not the Ones You Wish You Had)

Our high-pressure parenting culture gives lip service to the idea that we should love our children no matter what—love them as they are—but then drives us toward intensive interference with our kids, as though they are flawed and need to be highly crafted, repaired, and actively changed. Just as we looked at how to be present with yourself as you parent, let's look at what it is to also extend that acceptance and sense of "good enough" to your children—or, rather, to the part of your children that you may be embarrassed by or worried about or feel shame about.

Jessica, like many of us, loves her child, Robby, deeply. And she does not judge him. Or so she truly, truly thinks. But the more honest she was with herself, the more she realized that this was untrue—and she felt horrible about it!

Robby's behavior had been almost impossible to manage from the time he started walking, because he never stopped moving. "I think my parenting anxiety started when Robby was probably eighteen months old and I realized there was something going on," Jessica explained. By age two Robby was receiving occupational therapy for sensory processing disorder, and at age four Robby was appropriately diagnosed with severe ADHD.

"The hardest part for me was in public places, whether it was a store or a restaurant. I sometimes had to walk out of the grocery and leave a whole cart of food and stuff because he would get so overwhelmed and start screaming." Jessica never blamed Robby or was upset with him. "I understood his backstory, you know. I understood where he was coming from." But she always noticed the looks people gave her and imagined what they were thinking: "Why is your kid acting like that?"

Jessica felt terrible shame and anxiety about these incidents. "One time when we had just had the second baby, we went out to breakfast, and he stood up—he was so happy about his new boxers— and he pulled his pants down to advertise to everybody, 'Look at these boxers! They've got superheroes on it.' Some people thought it was funny, but an older couple in the corner was looking like, 'What is your child doing?'"

She knew she should ignore other people's looks and judgements; they didn't understand that he could experience sensory overload and that was why he might act differently. But even though she understood why he acted the way he acted, and that it was not his fault, there was a part of her that really wished he didn't act so weirdly.

"I know him. I know his story. But I don't ever want him to feel bad for who he is. So, I try not to give into it myself." So, she was in conflict—she wished he didn't have these behaviors and she felt awful for wishing that her child was different than he was.

The tremendous energy level and impulsivity of kids with ADHD can cause a lot of embarrassment. Those who witness these moments tend to assume that the adults aren't managing that child properly. And Jessica had somewhat internalized that, but knew she shouldn't. But she did. But felt she shouldn't. But she did.

However, after the drama, when the family was out of the restaurant and outside of the glare of judgment, Jessica was able to sigh, and she could easily see her son. "He has so much love, so much joy for things." Yes, Robby was impulsive and hyperactive and, in some cases, safety was a real concern. But his joyfulness and zest for life were inseparable from who he was, and she truly loved that.

Being able to see things that she valued even in his "weird" moments informed Jessica's goals for how she approached raising him. "I'm not going to keep him from struggling in his life. But I want to make sure he knows he has support." Other people might judge him, and she might even feel uncomfortable about some of the startling things he does, but the same impulsivity that made him drop his shorts in a restaurant also injected a joy and energy that she loved.

As Jessica continued using Sigh, See, Start, she began to manage her own parenting anxiety by focusing on the progress Robby was making over time. "My anxiety sometimes gets the best of me. I will replay something in my head a million times over. And people say 'Oh, just let it go, let it go.' And truly, you can't just let it go." But then she would sigh and remind herself, "You're along for the ride and try to do the best you can to make it through." And then she would start "trying to think where to go from there." Often that led her to consider what really mattered to her as a parent. If she heard about a day at school when her son's learning wasn't the best, but he had been able to participate well in activities and done well socially, then she was happy, because that was her goal for him at this age and what they were working on in therapy. And she truly amazed me when she explained that now when something happened at the grocery store, she focused on seeing Robby and how he was doing and if he was overstimulated. She didn't worry about the looks she was getting.

Achievement Culture

There are few things our culture is better at than holding up an unreachable ideal and telling us it's normal, be it in parenting at home or in the workplace. But when you look closely at the people who are held up as examples, as idols, it becomes clear that while they may be ideal in one sense, it is at the cost of some other part of their being. They've sacrificed growth in some areas of the human experience to maximize others. Luminaries of achievement like Bill Gates and

Tiger Woods have all sorts of trouble in their personal relationships. There is a popular meme by an unknown author that justly identifies the problem with achievement culture: "If a child can do advanced math, speak three languages, or receive top grades, but can't manage their emotions, practice conflict resolution, or handle stress, none of that other stuff is really going to matter."

While many parents get pulled into achievement culture and prioritize that over other elements of their child's development, other parents know that kids need rich emotional skills. The former are particularly burnt out, as they try to practice a popular style of intensive emotional coaching and support, while also making sure their kids achieve, easily falling into a confusing mix of over-nurturing alternating with pushing. Why? Because that's what happens when you try to reach an impossible standard that is out of sync with the reality of your situation. Full disclosure: my tendency is to join the second group of parents.

The Family You Have

To truly give our kids what they need, we must consider the family dynamic as a whole, instead of an individual child out of context. As parents, we often focus so wholeheartedly on one child that we neglect our own needs and/or the needs of whichever child is less needy at the time. Of course, there are times of crisis when this is unavoidable, such as when a child is newly diagnosed with an illness, but such a response is meant to be time-limited or it has lasting consequences for everyone. We are not meant to parent like we are in crisis all the time. That's unbalanced and unhealthy. Is it worth feeding the family fast food five nights a week and giving up on exercise for ourselves and the younger kids, who get excessive screen time in the family van, to drive the talented child to their dance team so they can pursue their passion? Only you can make that choice; to make it with intention, consider the whole family, not just one member or goal.

Kids do best when they are in a family where everyone's needs matter and are tended to. As frustrated parents have pointed out to me many times, parenting advice seems to assume that we are working one on one with a single child at a time, equipped with an endless amount of patience, energy, and wisdom. From a Sigh, See, Start viewpoint, when we think about raising our family, we take into account all the kids and caregivers involved. As a parent, my instinct and my belief are always to put my kids first over my own needs, but if I am routinely depleting myself, am I taking care of the family unit as best I can? A thriving mom's presence wins out over a depleted mom's every time.

In modern families we often live in multiple households, with parents, co-parents, foster parents, grandparents, and other caregivers, all of whom are involved in the dynamics of the family. Or we may be single parents and their helpers (or lack thereof). Instead of one parent and one child, the word *family* helps us to acknowledge the way dynamics between children, as well as between us, our children, and other caregivers can throw a wrench into our attempts to provide perfectly unruffled ideal parenting.

Parents are constantly sharing with me their sense of failure because they can't live up to the idealized and unrealistic model our culture gives us: that we are meant to come to parenting as finished adults with all our stuff together and then impart our wisdom to our fragile children. But that's not how it works. When we become parents we join a new system, a family. And rather than having all the knowledge we need, we quickly discover that we are learning through experience. That's the only way truly to learn when it comes to people. Raising the family you have embraces this reality of family development and family growth. It rejects an unrealistic view that it's only the children who are developing. We are constantly influencing each other; sometimes we are growing together and sometimes we are hindering each other's growth. With this perspective, we can see the times when we don't know what to do not as a failure, but as a completely normal opportunity for family development and growth. We can stop pretending we ought to know things we couldn't possibly ever know, and approach this parenting journey with our families with new eyes, full of wonder and curiosity. A little flexibility and room not to know makes room for growth, while insisting on certainty can nip it in the bud. Because whether we like it or not, our kids and the adults in our family system will keep growing and changing. We can either be responsive to it or be resistant to it, but we can't stop it.

The Wonder of It All

Being present in our reality brings us within reach of one of the most inspiring aspects of being human: the experience of awe and wonder. That feeling of reverential mind-expanding wonder is something most of us experience or associate with places like the Grand Canyon or ancient monuments like Machu Picchu or the Egyptian pyramids. But it's also the experience of an infinite number of parents the first time they look in their newborns' eyes. Awe makes us feel like we stepped out of time, like we're part of something so much more, like we're at the peak of existence. It's not something we expect to feel in the course of our daily existence, but, in fact, it is available to all of us.

Part of approaching parenting with a Sigh, See, Start mindset is remembering to savor the wonder our children inspire in us. We can change our perspectives and feed our souls, giving us a bit more of the strength we need to engage with our situation today, especially when it's hard, and to continue our growth as parents tomorrow. According to one scholarly paper, "Awe-inducing events may be one of the fastest and most powerful methods of personal change and growth."[82]

The Benefits of Awe

Scientific studies on awe have found an impressive list of benefits: Awe makes us feel happier and increases our positive emotions. It makes us more curious and creative and brings feelings of connectedness with a greater desire to help others. Awe changes the way we feel and helps us savor our feelings and physical sensations. It also produces higher-level cognitive processing and brings more open-minded and deeper insights. Awe has also been found to reduce stress, loneliness, anxiety, depression, and pain.[83]

The most impressive impact of awe is the way it changes our perception of time. Time actually expands, and our normal mundane concerns fade. Jake Eagle, whose work on micro-moments of mindfulness we looked at in Chapter 5, believes this is the key feature of awe: that sense of timelessness makes us feel more patient, and that patience brings our best attributes to the surface. Imagine what it would feel like if you had all the time in the world. How much pressure would that relieve?

Fortunately, Eagle and his coauthor of the book *The Power of Awe*, Michael Amster, a pain medicine specialist, created a method that helped people get all the benefits of awe by practicing it for five to twenty-five seconds a few times a day. That sounds doable for busy parents, and the practice itself is very similar to Sigh, See, Start.

THE A.W.E. METHOD

───

→ *Attention:* Turn your full and undivided attention to things you appreciate, value, or find amazing. Instead of forcing yourself to focus, let your attention float into appreciation.

→ **Wait:** Slow down and pause. Continue your attention for at least one deep inhale.

→ **Exhale and Expand:** When you breathe out slowly, about twice the length of your inhale (similar to sighing), you begin to relax and amplify whatever sensations you are experiencing.

Try combining the A.W.E. method with Sigh, See, Start: Sigh and bring yourself into connection with your body, see what you appreciate, value, or find amazing, and then start floating into the experience, letting it expand by repeatedly sighing and seeing.

You can do this with anything. Of course, my favorite subjects are my kids and my dogs, because they are so often cute and delightful. You will know when you are experiencing awe because of the physical changes, such as goosebumps, shivers, chills, or a release of energy. You may feel more alert and notice your vision is clearer. And your facial expression may change, with a smile, wide eyes, raised eyebrows, and a relaxed jaw. This is because the A.W.E. method is another way to regulate your nervous system. As someone who had been practicing meditation for years, I can echo what Amster said about his method: "I feel like the state of peace and being that I sought for over thirty years as a meditator is something I can find in just a few breaths. I am able to instantaneously change my state of consciousness and experience profound presence and peace that filters throughout my entire day."[84]

When you let the wonder of your child wash over you, the nagging worries of parenting loosen their grip as you remember what an astonishing miracle it is to be entrusted with this child. It's not that your worries aren't important; it's just that they pale in comparison to reality of your child. You know this already. You felt this when they were born, until the hectic pace of life distracted you. But when you let the practice of awe remind you of what you know about your child, you radiate that love for and confidence in your child — and they are nurtured.

The Importance of Family Development

We've all heard of child development: that it follows a trajectory with milestones that typically occur at certain times. Often, parents don't realize that they are developing, too, or, even worse, they actually feel bad about it because they've been misled into thinking that they are supposed to come to parenting as fully finished all-wise adults. However, parenthood is constantly full of new situations as our children surprise us with how rapidly they change and how different they are from us. As Andrew Solomon writes, "All offspring are startling to their parents."[85] How, then, can we not be growing and developing ourselves? When we're honest with ourselves, we know that our children have a special talent for revealing the places where we need to grow.

If we think in terms of raising the family we have, meaning we are raising ourselves right along with our children, suddenly being a parent seems a lot more fun. Consider how beautiful it is that we are all growing together and influencing each other while we do. We are given this amazing opportunity to grow and gain wisdom ourselves, even as we shepherd our children through their development. And the more we truly listen to our children, and appreciate their viewpoints, the more we grow. It's not a one-way interaction where parents drop their wisdom on the kids. Rather, it's a human experience: just as our nervous systems are constantly interacting with each other, so are our minds growing along with each other.

Raising the family you have as an articulation of a Sigh, See, Start mindset means that you root what you do in the reality of your circumstances without burning yourself out, and you make room to develop what our ShouldStorm prevents—the deepest and richest level of human experience—and share it as a family.

CHAPTER 6 : KEY TAKEAWAYS

- In order to leave the ShouldStorm, we need a Sigh, See, Start mindset of strength, confidence, and presence.
- Sigh, See, Start lets us be present with how things are and then do what makes sense.
- We all have an energy envelope, and it's okay not to constantly push ourselves too hard.
- One articulation of a Sigh, See, Start mindset is to think about raising the family you have.
- The word *raising* implies that kids have their own strengths and need room to develop without intensive parental interference.
- We can love and accept the kids we have, not the kids we think we should have.
- Families, meaning parents and kids, are growing and developing along with each other.
- Practicing mini-moments of awe can restore our peace and joy as parents.

Chapter 7

Connecting from the Heart

Emotional regulation flows naturally from being in the presence of someone we trust.
—Bonnie Badenoch, *The Heart of Trauma: Healing the Embodied Brain in the Context of Relationships*

The foundation of our parenting relationship must be connection and trust. If our kids don't feel able to be open with us about who they are, we can neither enjoy them nor influence them. And kids want this, too: they often tell me how much they value it when their parents take time to understand them and the closeness it brings.

In this chapter we'll learn about tools that can help us get to that place of trust and connection more easily and more often. We will look at the work of psychologist Richard Schwartz on Internal Family Systems (IFS) and how self-regulating our own autonomic nervous systems (ANS) allows us to co-regulate with our children. By combining these models with Sigh, See, Start, we will become more present and capable in our interactions, even as we parent from that mindset of abundance and confidence.

IFS and Understanding Parts

When psychologist Richard Schwartz, now affiliated with the department of psychiatry at Harvard Medical School, was a young family therapist, he hit a wall with clients who had eating disorders. None of the methods he had trained in were helping them, so he eventually let go of his assumptions and simply started listening to his clients. When he did, he began to observe a surprising pattern: his clients were all talking about different parts of themselves, such as inner critics, or parts that felt lonely, or parts that would soothe them by binge eating, only for the critic to come back and berate them for binging. "So I became intrigued, and I began to try to track these sequences.... And then I started noticing that I had them too."[86]

It's an experience we've all had when we might say, "Part of me wants to eat that cake, but another part wants to stick to my health goal," or even, "Part of me knows I did the best I could, but my inner critic won't stop yelling at me."

Schwartz called the different sub-personalities inside us "parts," the word his clients used. While the idea of parts of the personality or sub-personalities has been explored by many others, the unique finding came when Schwartz noticed that the parts seemed to interact like a family. His training was now paying off, and he used some of the techniques he'd used to get family members talking to each other with his clients. Except this time, he had them talk to themselves on the inside. He called his new model of psychology Internal Family Systems (IFS).[87]

But the discovery that came next was the most amazing. When Schwartz began using family communication techniques with his clients' parts, something unexpected emerged. Every single person attested to a peaceful place inside them that they called "themselves." And the more that self emerged and interacted with their parts, the more healing they experienced. Schwartz called it the Self with a capital S and found it contained all the best qualities a person could have, a list we'll review below.

When we consider how parts work, the more extreme behaviors we see in ourselves or our kids make more sense. Our parts take on one of three jobs: to hold our pain for us so we don't have to feel it, to prevent us from feeling that pain, and to stop pain once it starts.[88] The parts performing that third action, who will do anything to stop pain, are the ones that shock us with behaviors that seem so out of character for us, like screaming at a loved one, trashing a room, soothing with binge eating, or totally shutting down and withdrawing.

The Pixar movie *Inside Out* illustrates parts beautifully. In the movie we get to ride around in the control room of the brain of a young girl named Riley as her sub-personalities work to keep her safe and happy. The movie gets exciting when those parts, namely Fear, Anger, Joy, Disgust, and Sadness, start fighting for control. Joy tries to focus on the positive, even when it means denying Riley's experiences, and manages Riley's behavior to keep it acceptable to others. But when things get tough, other parts use less acceptable or more extreme behaviors to protect her. When Fear is in the lead, Riley cringes. When it's Anger, she explodes into unkind speech toward her parents. The same sort of process goes on inside her parents' heads, too. From the inside out, we see everyone's behavior with compassion, not as simplistic black-or-white, right-or-wrong choices, but as a more complicated effort to do the best they can in a tough situation. You and your kids have good intentions. But sometimes those good intentions are expressed in problematic ways.

Parents and Their Parts

Have you ever reacted to your child in a way you regretted? Have you shut them down, or become very angry and shamed them?

Frank Anderson, a psychiatrist and psychologist who has spent his career helping children and adults with trauma, explains the role parts take in parents: "Anytime you get triggered, anytime you have an intense reaction, it's not about your kids. It's about you and your history. And are you willing and able to take a look at that?"[89] That's not easy, given that IFS teaches us that our parts work together to make sure we avoid connecting with the pain of our histories.

And it's not just our own parts that do this: our parent friends have a way of insulating us from taking full responsibility for ourselves as well. We say, "Let's not judge parents and be hard on them because it's a really hard job." But Anderson finds that giving parents permission to lose it, as if that's in the normal range, is allowing a pattern that's not good for kids. In my own observation, parents often carry so much shame that we oscillate between intense self-criticism and justifying ourselves by blaming it on our kids (in order to avoid feeling our shame). This is because we know the truth of what Anderson told me next, "Yes, everybody loses it. And every time you do, your kid loses a safe parent, and you have the responsibility to repair that."[90]

Repair is a subject we explored in Chapter 4, but Schwartz explains briefly in the context of IFS,

> So you're going to get upset with your kid. And you're going to lose it, and you're going to shame them at times.... But after it happens, if you're aware of it, and you catch it, then you could also go back to the kid and say, "You know, I'm aware that this part of me just took over, and I am sorry that I let that happen. And my job as a parent is not to let that happen, so I'm going to work on it. And you still have to get up on time and go to school."[91]

As parents, we can use these times to explore our parts and understand why we reacted so strongly to our child, so hopefully it doesn't keep happening. "By triggering you, your kid is letting you know what you need to heal, rather than what you need to feel ashamed of or try to…suppress," says Schwartz.[92]

The language of IFS helps us make sense of our conscious experiences and our behavior in a non-shaming way. As parents, we spend most of our time living like managers, one of the most valued parts in our culture: we watch the clock, we stay on task, and we use our analytical minds to make sure everybody does what they should be doing. There is absolutely a time and a place for this: we all have to manage the world we live in and train our kids to manage it, too. But as modern life keeps speeding up and we have less time to do anything but stay on task, we pay a price. Without time when we are not expected to be doing anything, we lose our connections to our deeper selves, so much so that we may forget that Self, the "real us," even exists. Yet that is the person whose presence our children want and need.

For parents who have experienced trauma of their own, particularly if it happened in childhood, their true selves can be particularly difficult to access. We adapt by adopting a set of behaviors (or by forming parts) that manage our emotions and experiences to keep us away from anything that triggers our trauma memories. But by avoiding our deeper hurt places, we always avoid what makes us us. And by the time we become parents, avoiding triggers becomes impossible: we will inevitably be triggered by our own children, or simply by the shame and criticism of the ShouldStorm.

When our kids show us where we need to heal or grow, we can get to work, bringing our selves to our parts and listening to them with compassion and curiosity. IFS also gives us a deeper perspective on repair—the idea that even if we ourselves were abused, even if we ourselves have reenacted some of what was done to us, deep inside ourselves and our children is healing Self-energy. This doesn't mean we do it alone—trauma rewires our brains in a way that must be

addressed with the right help and a good trauma-trained therapist —
but healing is definitely possible for parents who recognize their own
pain and don't want to pass it on.

The Self in IFS

Theories of mindfulness, schools of psychology, such as the
"wise mind" in dialectical behavioral therapy, and religions the
world over have long spoken of the soul or Self, an entity that is
beyond behavior and that is able to be present with all that we are.
IFS proposes that when this Self is present, you can see your individual parts as parts, as an angry part or a scared part; with the
space this provides, the Self can be curious about the parts and their
behaviors — it can take responsibility for them or relate to them in
all manner of ways. You have an essential Self that is bigger than
you think, that is big enough to have all you need to parent and
live well.

Even though our culture has done a thorough job of convincing parents that we are deficient, the truth is exactly the opposite.
No matter how hard life has been, including loss or trauma, parents
already have what they need within themselves. Schwartz observes
that everyone has a Self, which he calls our "birthright," equipped
with everything we need. When a person is able to access that Self
and interact with the world from that core place, wonderful qualities show up naturally. We don't have to work for or earn those
qualities, because we already have them.

That means that as parents we come equipped with what our
kids needs most. Schwartz describes the qualities of Self in quite a
list. There are the eight Cs: calmness, clarity, compassion, curiosity, confidence, courage, creativity, and connectedness. And the five
Ps: presence, patience, perspective, persistence, and playfulness.
"All those combine to make a good parent, and all of that is already

there. And so, [parenting] isn't a matter of learning something they don't know. It's a matter of working with what gets in the way of that," Schwartz told me.[93]

How, then, can we access this Self and bring it to our kids? One of the best ways I know is to simply ask yourself whether you have an agenda in that moment. If you're mainly curious, engaged, and interested, then you are coming from your true Self and your kids will feel it. For those of us who are used to the constant doing of modern life, it comes as a surprise how much ease showing up from our selves brings to our relationships with our kids, as the Self naturally makes room for whoever they are at that time.

Understanding Your Kids' Parts

IFS helps us to see our children's behavior in a whole new light. Old-school ideas about behavior still influence us and create a lot of confusion in our culture about what behavior means. In this way of thinking, when a person who has always been kind to you says something mean, it must mean they are revealing their true character—they were never actually a kind person and they can be written off. This belief was part of what drove most parents to spank their children: in order to save your child from being a bad person, you must beat the bad behavior out of them.

With the language of parts, we can recognize that we all have different parts, and that our bad behavior comes from a good intention: it's meant to protect us by preventing pain or trying to get us something we think we need. IFS tells us that we have a core Self that is good, even when we do bad things. It makes space for us to fearlessly take responsibility for our actions and seek repair. Because we have a deeper Self to draw on, we can survive the guilt we must face when we take responsibility and are then able to generate healing, joy, and growth inside us.

IFS changes our understanding of our own and our kids' behavior, allows for healing instead of correction, and increases our awareness of our own abilities. Instead of muscling through and "managing" behaviors with willpower, we can pivot into the courageous curiosity of our deeper selves, opening up an opportunity for everyone to grow. You have different parts and also a deeper Self with its own wisdom, and so do your kids. Understanding how parts work allows you to understand what's going on inside yourself better. It also helps you take a different view of your kids. Instead of judging your child's behavior, you can ask, "What need is my child trying to meet with this behavior? What developmental strategy might they be trying?"

However, unless you've worked with an IFS group or therapist, knowing how to bring that Self-energy online can be very challenging for parents, especially under pressure. In the rest of this chapter we'll look at how to use our nervous systems to help our best selves emerge, and then to use those selves to bring out the best in our kids.

Accessing Our Best Selves through the Nervous System

If parts and selves describe our conscious experience, the autonomic nervous system (ANS) is the preconscious platform that drives that experience. As we first learned in Chapter 5, outside of conscious awareness, higher brain circuits continuously scan our environment for signs of safety or danger. When safety is detected, the calming ventral vagal circuit promotes sociality and healthy body function. However, when a threat is detected, the brainstem's survival circuits reflexively shift the ANS into a state of defense, without us making a conscious decision about it. According to Deb Dana, a therapist and author who uses both IFS and the polyvagal theory (PVT) of the ANS to help her clients, what state our nervous system is in determines what parts of us show up, or when our true Self can be present.[94]

As we learned in Chapter 5, Sigh, See, Start offers a simple way to practice moving flexibly between the states of our ANS. As a reminder, the ANS puts us in three different states, driven by three different nerve branches: when we feel safe we are in the social nervous system driven by the ventral vagus nerve, when we detect a threat we move into the mobilization/fight-or-flight response driven by the sympathetic nerve, and when we feel overwhelming threat we move into the immobilization/freeze-or-faint response mediated by the dorsal vagus nerve. By recognizing times when we are in a state of defense and self-regulation, we can access our social nervous system—which is when our best Self shows up. However, when we are fully in fight-or-flight or freeze-or-faint, the areas of our brain that enable us to be self-aware are shut off, and that makes it hard to self-regulate. Opportunity comes in the brief moments of clarity when we think, "I just yelled in impatience," or, "I just completely shut them out when they were trying to connect." Those moments are when we can sigh, a few times if needed, sending signals of safety to our body and noticing what we are feeling, whether it's anxiety, anger, or heaviness and disconnection. Then see your child and your situation, noticing what might be making you feel unsafe. The threat might be something as simple as feeling you should be able to control your child's behavior and you can't, or feeling inadequate or disrespected.

Here's where it gets tricky. If you act too quickly, you may still be reacting to a should that says, "I should not have yelled" or "I should connect." As long as you are acting out of a should you are still in a state of defense, one of your self-protective parts is in charge, and you are reacting to the unsafe feeling you have of failure. Instead, keep sighing until you feel an opening up of your desire to connect without that driven feeling of needing to fix something. Then start bringing your warmth, calm, and compassion to your child. We'll learn some practical ways to do that below.

When Monique was first practicing the sigh step, she noticed that her husband had been using it with her for some time. One time, she had been listing her worries to him about whether their daughter was in enough activities or missing out, and he simply looked at her and took deep breaths. "I remember he just sucked in and pushed out and didn't say anything," Monique said. She found herself breathing with him, and asking herself, "Why am I putting that on her?" In that moment, Monique and her husband were co-regulating.

Using Our Nervous System to Help Regulate Our Child

Self-regulation is important for parents for two reasons: first, we can only show up as the connected parent our kids need when we are in a regulated and calm state, and second, because self-regulating allows us to co-regulate our kids. Co-regulation means that a parent who is in a regulated state themselves, generally in the social nervous system, uses their state to send signals of safety to their child. In this way, a parent may either help their child stay regulated or soothe their dysregulated child back into a regulated state where they can learn or respond to what their parent asks of them.

Psychologist Tina Payne Bryson and her coauthor, neuroscientist and professor of psychiatry Daniel J. Seigel, have written a series of books together starting with *The Whole-Brain Child*, with the goal of convincing parents that co-regulation is the key to helping children develop a secure attachment. "Co-regulation is one of our primary functions as mammals to better ensure the survival of our young," Bryson told me. "We are attuned to their stressed states, physical or emotional, and we work to regulate those stressed states so they don't go into fight, flight, or freeze." Without co-regulation, infants can go into high states of physiological arousal from simple things like hunger or not being comfortable with the temperature.

Co-regulation helps keep their "little nervous systems from being flooded with stress hormones."[95]

The reality is that whether we recognize it or not, "our nervous systems are the ones that are always in conversation," said Dana.[96] The two-way nature of this means that when a parent is aware of which state they are in, they are able to notice if a child's provocation has shifted them from a sense of safety to fight-or-flight, for example. That self-awareness — "Uh oh, I'm in a triggered state" — can be an important data point for the parent as they choose their behavior. Perhaps they notice how quickly they get furious and realize, I need to take a breath before I reply. Or maybe the parent is too triggered and yells like a wild thing at their kid, only to realize after the fact that they crossed a line. Whether the parent noticed the state before or after losing it, the awareness is an asset: they can either avoid the harsh behavior (if they are able to assess their state and manage it beforehand) or they can aim for repair with their child if they notice it after the fact. But without the awareness, there is only disconnection and hurt without the solace of repair.

This means that we can't give our child the co-regulation they need unless we practice ANS regulation ourselves. A healthy nervous system makes use of its different states when needed and moves flexibly between them. If your child is hitting and screaming and biting you, a healthy nervous system would send you an alarm signal by activating the mobilized state of the sympathetic nerve. But that activated nervous system doesn't have to be an automated, angry system: we can use Sigh, See, Start to self-regulate even under pressure and model responses for our children.

According to Bryson, co-regulation is one of the best ways to build the brain. By repeatedly soothing our children's distressed states, we are building our children's brains' ability to get back into a regulated state and therefore to learn to trust their environment and to trust their caregivers. "It's like when we lift weights and do reps, those muscles get stronger when caregivers provide co-regulation. It can give their nervous systems reps and build their brain's ability to do that for themselves."[97]

Co-regulation is something we need throughout our lifetime to a varying degree, but by the time kids are in high school they are able to self-regulate most of the time. Still, Bryson said co-regulation continues to build their brains. "It helps wire their mental models for reaching out and connecting with people when they're having a hard time."[98]

By the time kids are older, parents, especially those raised in old-school ways themselves, may lose patience with all the soothing and think, "Aren't they old enough to just do what they are supposed to do without all this emotional effort on my part?" "Yes," said Bryson, "we're all supposed to be doing what we're supposed to be doing all the time. But we don't, particularly when we're in high emotional states and we're not regulated."[99] Because adolescents have very rapidly developing brains, they are more emotionally volatile, and this means that co-regulation remains very important. When parents offer their presence to help kids feel safe, seen, soothed, and secure, they are acting like an external brain with a functioning prefrontal cortex (the part of the brain responsible for higher-level thinking, which shuts down during states of defense), helping the child's brain do what it cannot do until it moves back into a regulated state.

And contrary to what parents might have been taught, Bryson emphasized that co-regulation is actually one of the best ways to get cooperation. When children are having a tantrum, or a big emotional response, or, "They're being oppositional and they don't want to do what they need to do, like get their shoes on and get in the car, or do their homework, that's when we co-regulate," said Bryson. "We often don't have choices about our behavior in those states."

When our kids are stressed (fight-or-flight) or depressed (shut down), their higher brain (or prefrontal cortex) is shut down. They simply cannot pause, look at options, consider consequences, have empathy for others or have personal insight, be mindful, give attuned communication, or make good decisions, according to Bryson. But that happens to be precisely when we parents get frustrated and start demanding that our kids solve their problems or make decisions wisely. Rather than butting heads with our kids, our goal is to bring them into a state where they can work with us by sending their nervous systems the cues of safety they're watching for. "It's when they're at their worst that they need us most," said Bryson.

All of this explains why shaming and blaming, especially of older kids and teens who we think should be able to do what we ask, is so ineffective. It also sends them a terrible message, namely, "You shouldn't come to me when you're in distress. I'm only interested in being in a relationship with you when you're in a regulated state, which is the exact opposite of what we want to communicate in the hardest times," said Bryson. If our kids can't trust us with their small moments of stress, they won't come to us for the big ones.

When our kids are being "difficult" and pushing us away, they may secretly be more vulnerable and open to connection with us. "There are amazing, wonderful opportunities to show up in those moments and to provide at least the offer of co-regulation," she said. Bryson suggested saying things like I understand, I want to give you your space, I'll be right downstairs, I'll always listen if you need me.[100] Even if co-regulation hasn't been on your radar, it's never too late to start. The brain is neuroplastic and can rewire itself based on experience.

The Pressure to Be Calm All the Time.

It's all too easy to take this advice too far, expecting absolutely perfect calm in yourself as a parent to avoid ever sending your child any message of unsafety. Some parents get the incorrect message that if their child is "acting up" it's because they have failed to co-regulate well enough. Pressure like this comes from the ShouldStorm, and pushes parents right past co-regulation into the opposite: invasive over-nurturing, which is when a dysregulated parent dysregulates their child further in order to avoid shame.

As Jessica Winter points out in her analysis for the *New Yorker* of a new style of overparenting sometimes referred to as "gentle parenting," the idea that all of children's "challenging behavior is a physiological response to stress and should be seen as essentially adaptive" can't explain everything, all of the time. "If little Timmy is on the front lawn tossing gardening implements at traffic, his motivations are probably obscurer than stress…. Sometimes a child tests or destroys boundaries for the thrill of it," she writes.[101] This is of course true: Timmy might be in a mixed state of play, when both the mobilization response and the social nervous system are online. Play is the state where we can enjoy our friends jumping out and scaring us during a game of tag. Or Timmy might simply be imitating something he saw on YouTube.

Because there are many factors that inform a child's behavior, we can use Sigh, See, Start to parent our child in the moment. There is no one factor or approach to understanding your child. But understanding the way our nervous system informs our behavior is a great addition to our toolbox: suddenly a whole lot of our own and our kids' behaviors start to make more sense.

Kids Who Struggle

Some kids can get pretty extreme when they are dysregulated, particularly kids who are neuro-atypical and have learning disabilities, sensory sensitivities, or mood disorders. When kids have major meltdowns, scream, yell, or even cause property damage, it's extremely hard to stay regulated yourself. Parents who have experienced extreme behavior from a child can benefit from creating a plan for times they become dysregulated themselves.

Let's say your child is screaming and yelling and slamming doors; then they break something and you find yourself losing it. You are yelling at them to stop and things escalate. When you have that fleeting moment of sanity that says, "Oh, no, I'm losing it," as long as your child is safe from harming themselves, or they're old enough, it's okay to take a little break from each other. It's better to let things cool down than to engage in a pointless power struggle. In the next chapter, we'll look at a problem-solving method that can help to prevent some of these moments ahead of time.

HOW TO USE SIGH, SEE, START TO CO-REGULATE

SIGH: Bring yourself into connection with your own nervous system and activate your ventral vagus nerve.

SEE: Notice your child's state. Which one (or mix of two) of the following might they be experiencing?

→ *Social engagement:* Do they appear calm, open, and receptive? Are their faces expressive? Are they making eye contact easily? Do their voices sound melodic?

→ *Mobilized:* Do they seem tense? Are their eyes staring more intensely? Do their voices sound flat or irritated? Are they moving in an agitated way? Are they arguing with or avoiding you?

→ *Immobilized:* Do they have a flat facial expression without a sense of peace to it? Are their eyes blank? Is there a lack of eye contact? Are they staring off into space? Are they still and not moving, but not relaxed? Do you ask yourself, "Where did they go?"

START: If your child is socially engaged, proceed with your parenting activity while communicating safety. If they are in one of the states of defense, start offering cues of safety. You'll learn over time what works best for your child in each state. These ideas can get you started: If your child is mobilized (in fight-or-flight), stop. It may be time to try something else. Maintain a respectful distance because intensity in your voice or touching your child can be threatening to them. However, there are a minority of children who respond well to being hugged deeply and held until they are calm. You might offer calming words with a musical gentle voice. Instead of saying, "Calm down," or, "Stop it," which just seems to annoy people further, try saying, "I'm right here with you. I'm here to help you." If a child is in a complete meltdown, it is certainly okay to ask them to stop damaging property or hurting themselves with a calm voice, but often the only effective approach is to stay close enough to prevent them from truly harming themselves while keeping your distance and waiting until the storm blows over.

What doesn't work is telling kids in this state to quiet down or sit still. According to Deb Dana, our bodies need to move when in the mobilized state, which is why we tell kids to go outside to play. The mobilized state is characterized by disorganized movement, which is why Dana offers a number of tools that channel that need to move into more organized movements. "As soon as we allow movement that is within some sort of structure rather than random or disorganized, the nervous system starts to come into regulation," said Dana. Examples include: rocking chairs or gliders, or sitting on a physio ball because it "invites movement while staying present."[102] In my family, we've found that having the kids do pushups or carry heavy objects can help, because it also involves the heavy work that sends a deep pressure stimulus to the vagus nerve.

Dana also keeps a bottle of bubble stuff in her office, for both kids and adults, because blowing bubbles is impossible without the long slow exhalation that calms our nervous system. She also recommends parents try a kazoo, if they can stand the noise, because kids have to control their breath to play a kazoo. Over time, when kids have had more practice learning regulation techniques, they may become willing to simply sigh along with you.

Playing music or singing with your child can also help, because singing combines both breath control and using that melodic voice that tells our nervous system we are safe. In fact, Disney music is particularly effective because it is almost all recorded in the medium range of the human voice, which is what we sound like when the social nervous system is active. For about a year after I learned about PVT, I used to turn on the *Moana* soundtrack whenever my boys started arguing and I couldn't break it up. It was like magic. Within a minute they would both calm down, and (usually) sort it out.

Touch or deep pressure can help tremendously, but I do not recommend this until your child has reached a point of partial calm. For kids who can express themselves verbally, try asking them if they would like their back rubbed, or a hug, or to have you play with their hair. Do not touch them until they are ready. If you hug them, ask them how tight they would like you to hug them, and follow their lead. Hugging is tremendously valuable when kids are ready, because it not only calms the ANS, but it releases oxytocin, the love and bonding hormone.

For homes with pets, few things bring us back into regulation faster than playing with or snuggling with a beloved animal. Because higher mammals have a similar social nervous system to our own, dogs, cats, and guinea pigs can be particularly helpful in co-regulating with us.

If your child is immobilized (freeze/faint): When people are first learning how to move out of the immobilized state, Dana emphasized that there is only one method that helps: "In the beginning, you really need somebody to join with you. Because when you go to dorsal [vagus nerve activation], you really feel like you're all alone in the world. You're lost. You're floating out there somewhere untethered. You need somebody to say, 'Okay, come on back. I'm here with you.' That's the language of the nervous system in dorsal. It's I'm here with you. I'm not going anywhere." Stay by your child in as calm and patient a state as you can maintain, and express that you are there in a gentle voice. Many parents also express their presence through touch, but be aware that touch is both a powerful regulator and dysregulator of the nervous system. So, closely observe your child's reaction and adjust what you are doing accordingly. Lastly, remember that pets are wonderful at expressing closeness when we are immobilized; my dogs and cat are always looking for a chance to sit on my lap and let me know they are with me.

WHAT TO AVOID WHEN LEARNING CO-REGULATION

→ *Avoid screens.* Few things calm kids down faster than handing them your phone, but recent research shows that using screens to calm children actually disrupts their ability to develop self-regulation.[103] This makes sense when we consider what we've learned in this chapter: children's nervous systems need social co-regulation to build those skills.

→ *Avoid rushed transitions.* Transitions are a tricky time when kids are already facing a challenging task for self-regulation, so trying to get them to interact or, worse, run the to-do list, can disrupt and make kids less willing to connect. The more kids experience us as dysregulating, the less they will be open to connecting.

→ *Avoid soothing a child with food, treats, or giving into demands*; these are shortcuts to avoid co-regulation. Just like screens, such methods may get in the way of a child learning to self-soothe over time. Co-regulation is simply using your state of calm to bring calm to your child. Sometimes that means holding a boundary until your child finishes fussing about it.

→ *Do not go it alone if your child has extreme or long-lasting meltdowns*. Please look at the tools in the next chapter on leadership, and also consider discussed options like occupational therapy (which teaches your child to notice what's going on with their body and provides the tools to calm it) with your pediatrician.

* * *

Connecting with our children from our best selves, understanding their behavior from a compassionate viewpoint, and helping them build a healthy nervous system through co-regulation represents much of what parenting with a Sigh, See, Start mindset is all about. However, stopping here could leave us with an unbalanced idea of what parenting looks like, which is why the next chapter explores using healthy leadership, expectations, and problem-solving to build our children's confidence.

CHAPTER 7 : KEY TAKEAWAYS

- Each of us has parts within that work to prevent pain or stop it once it starts.
- We are already equipped to be wonderful parents because we each have a true Self.
- The Self comes with built-in qualities, the eight Cs: calmness, clarity, compassion, curiosity, confidence, courage, creativity, and connectedness. And the five Ps: presence, patience, perspective, persistence, and playfulness.
- We can access our best selves by regulating our nervous systems.
- Co-regulation builds healthy nervous systems in our children and increases their ability to cooperate with us.

Chapter 8:

Building Confidence through Good Leadership

Researchers (and many parents!) have known for years that optimal development is most often established in predictable environments where children have an appropriate level of control.

—Karyn Purvis, *The Connected Parent*

We rarely think of parenting as leadership, and yet parents are the first and most influential leaders their children will ever have. However, parenting culture makes it hard to provide the kinds of steady leadership our children need because it strips us of our sense of confidence and control in favor of the ever-changing shoulds. Everyone needs leaders who can give them a sense of stability, but children, who are forming their sense of what to expect in the world, need that most of all. Embracing our role as leaders for our kids means strategically providing our kids the tools they need to live their lives with confidence. Good leaders believe in their kids' abilities; great leaders support their kids in growing those abilities. And that's what we'll learn how to do in this chapter, as we look at what leadership means within the framework of Sigh, See, Start.

Growing up in the 1980s and '90s led me to believe that all adolescents rebelled against their parents, denying their parents' very right to set rules for them at all. To my surprise, when I interviewed kids and teens for this book, I found that every single one of them welcomed their parents' rules. Ten-year-old Maddie, whose mother described her as incredibly responsible, capable, and independent, while simultaneously testing her parents, had no problem with her parents enforcing their rules. She told me that when her parents corrected her it was helpful because, "I'm trying to get me to be the best I can be." Similarly, when I asked nine-year-old Liam if it bothered him that adults were always deciding whether what he did was good enough, he cheerfully told me, "That's what parents are for." Teenagers tell me the same.

Certainly, I've talked to kids in my practice who resent their parents' expectations, but even these kids don't have a problem with the idea of parental authority; rather, they take issue with specific parental demands they find too hard, restrictive, or unfair. Today's kids attribute a fair amount of wisdom to their parents, even when they disagree on certain points. And this even includes kids I've worked with who are getting into trouble with drugs or risky behaviors, many of whom crave more leadership from their parents rather than less.

There are many definitions of good leadership, but I like to break it down into three tasks: setting expectations, coaching your team on how to reach those expectations, and cheering them on. One of the most effective ways I know to offer kids all three of these is the family meeting.

Family Meetings

Family meetings serve as a structured tool for providing leadership with Sigh, See, Start, because they are a time for everyone to come together in a relaxed way and talk about how things are going. During that discussion, each family member has an opportunity to practice seeing things in a new way or from a different person's perspective. Then the team can come together in starting something new. And these meetings are also a great time to model how to use Sigh, See, Start or explicitly teach it to your children.

Psychologist Barton Goldsmith writes, "In my years of practice [family meetings have] proven to be one of the most effective and bonding things families can do to create greater harmony and experience more depth and connection with those they love."[104] The precise structure and frequency of your family meetings is something you can adapt to your current situation and the maturity level of your children, but we found that even brief meetings were helpful when our kids were as young as two years old. Here's how to run a meeting with Sigh, See, Start:

→ *Sigh:* Get everybody together at a calm time and place when you can all relax. Bring yourself into a regulated state and suggest everyone sigh together a few times. Or, if you have eye-rolling adolescents like I do, simply sigh by yourself and watch everyone else unconsciously co-regulate and breathe along with you. Because you are the parent who called the meeting, your kids (and partner) will be watching you for signs they are in trouble, so they can't help but pick up on your calming cues.

Then ask everyone to take a moment to check in with themselves and ask how things are going as a family, or as an individual in the family.

→ *See:* This is a great moment to surprise your kids by flipping the usual order of leadership. Instead of starting with expectations, dive right in with affirmations. This is a time to share what you see about each person: praising the efforts they've put in, celebrating successes, thanking them for the things they do. Of particular importance is to point out how what they do impacts other family members. Organizational psychologist and professor at the Wharton School Adam Grant's research has found that people become easily discouraged in the workplace when they don't get to see how their work matters. However, Grant says, "Meeting one person helped by your work for five minutes was enough to almost double your effort and productivity."[105]

The same is true in families, which is why taking a moment to help our kids understand their impact while face to face with each other both affirms them and motivates them. Try saying, "I know it's a daily chore, but it really makes a difference to me when you clean up the kitchen every night. It's a relief to have one less thing to worry about." Or, "I really appreciated the way you went into your brother's room to cheer him up when he had a hard day. Moments like that really build each other up." This is a great way to start a meeting, and set a positive tone for all that follows.

Next, ask what people are seeing about what's working and what's not working. Be sure to express openness and curiosity and to invite everyone to share their viewpoints. When there are differences of opinion, encourage each other to imagine the other person's perspective. Even if your kids lack the maturity or patience to try, bringing this up sets a goal for our kids.

→ *Start:* When the family has identified an area that's not working, you've got an unsolved problem. In my house, we openly bring up areas of group friction in order to collaborate on solutions. Over time, our kids have grown confident that we really want to hear from them about times they feel we've been impatient or unfair, which offers us a chance to apologize and work with them on solutions. I have enjoyed observing how visibly this increases our kids' trust in us, and how that translates into less arguing about our expectations.

Because family meetings give our children a chance to understand the reasons behind our parenting actions and make their voices heard, they are less likely to get upset with them in the moment.

But problem-solving can be tricky, and we'll introduce a couple of tools to help solve these problems later in the chapter when we discuss the Collaborative and Proactive Solutions (CPS) method.

This is also a time to introduce "new business," such as new expectations or goals you'd like to set, or maybe fun things you've got planned. Be sure to offer an opportunity for your kids to suggest things they'd like to try, too, and collaborate with them.

By taking the lead and offering your children a space to have a voice and genuinely solve problems with you and each other, family meetings increase everyone's sense of belonging and value within the family. The Sigh, See, Start structure also allows us to communicate, or refine together, "clear roles and clear goals," something Grant has found to be even more important to team performance than interpersonal bonds. Without family meetings, it's easy for our kids to "only see their little corner of the puzzle, so they lose out on a sense of fitting in," as Grant says happens when leaders don't communicate a shared vision and mission. If you don't know what your family vision is, work with your kids and partners to clarify what it is. In general, the purpose of a family is to be a place where we can both give and receive belonging, love, safety, nurturing, and support. Then, as Grant says, make sure to communicate, "Here's why it matters, and here's the line of sight between what you do individually every day, and our collective purpose."[106]

Sometimes, we uncover problems that are not easily solved within a family meeting. These may be clues to more complex issues, such as a child with a developmental delay. Parents can make note of these concerns and follow up on them after the meeting, a subject we'll look at later in the chapter.

Regular parent or caregiver meetings, without the kids, can also be helpful. I truly believe our Friday night meetings were the only way my husband and I survived the busy years when our kids were very young. We learned to says things like, "Hey, I've noticed it works well with our kid when I do this," instead of, "You should do things the way I do."

HOW TO RUN A FAMILY MEETING

SIGH

• Help everyone into a calm and relaxed state.

SEE

• Start with affirmations.
• Invite kids to discuss key issues.

START

• Collaborate with your kids on solving the identified problems.
• After the meeting, follow up on more complex issues.

Delivering Affirmations

Cheering our children on isn't something that should happen only in family meetings. This is a crucial way to build our bond with our kids by offering them our presence and letting them know we see them. However, research shows that how we praise our kids matters. If we praise kids for the effort they put in, we encourage them to go for it. According to Carol Dweck, "Emphasizing effort gives a child a variable that they can control. They come to see themselves as in control of their success."[107]

In order to help your child feel felt, sigh to bring yourself into the present with your child, then see what they are doing, and then start praising their specific efforts. For example, say, "I love the way you used a number of different colors in that drawing. Can you tell me more about this area right here?" Showing interest and asking questions is one of the surest ways to build a child's sense of pride in their work, and even the youngest children can have some fascinating things to say about their scribbles. Or try combining praise with support by saying, "I notice that you worked really hard on your math homework here. Look how you figured out these questions. Remember, homework is practice so you can learn the material, and I see you got this problem wrong. I know you can figure this out. Let's look at it together." You can also use these moments both to communicate your own values and to affirm the child's personal goals. When my son was practicing his snare drum part for the middle school band, I said, "I felt very proud of you when you got frustrated learning your part and kept practicing anyway until you met your goal."

The more we teach our kids to focus on the times they do manage when they were initially unsure of what to do, the more confident they become about the future. Building confidence through praising effort is important for every child, but it is irreplaceable for kids with special needs or learning differences. Many of these kids spend a lot of time comparing themselves to others and feeling bad that they can't do certain things the way other people do. As parents, we try to comfort such children by saying things that rarely help, like, "Everyone is different, you can't compare yourself to others," or, "You are wonderful in your own way." These truths don't get at the source of our child's pain: the feeling that they can't do what the other kids can do. Instead, make a point to praise their efforts and especially times they solve problems in a way that works for them.

Kids can be ingenious about finding workarounds for their difficulties or disabilities, and when they do, discuss your admiration for what they did. If a child insists that this is evidence of what is wrong with them, point out that it is actually evidence of creativity. A Sigh, See, Start mindset means taking ourselves and our situations as they are and then finding what works for us, and when our kids do this they've practiced a crucial life skill.

What we want to avoid when cheering our kids on is praising them for things that they can't control. For example, research shows that kids who are praised for being "smart" end up avoiding challenges because they think that failing would show everyone they were not smart after all.[108] Even worse, praising kids for being smart actually makes them more likely to cheat, and that includes instances when they've overheard a classmate being called smart.[109] Cheating shows that a child has lost confidence in their own ability to tackle the test.

Solving Problems

One of the key steps in our family meeting is leading a dialogue about problems, which generally arise around spoken and unspoken expectations. As parents, our expectations are involved in virtually every interaction we have with our children, because they encompass everything from daily schedules, bedtimes, chores, how we treat each other, learning and schoolwork, and even sports and enrichment activities. We trust leaders (and kids trust parents) when they make us feel safe because we know what they expect, their expectations make sense, and they care about our perspective.

Child psychologist Ross Greene believes that parental expectations are the key to understanding our children's undesirable behaviors. "Kids exhibit concerning behaviors in response to very specific expectations that they are having trouble meeting," he told me in an interview. "That means we really shouldn't be focused on the concerning behavior and trying to modify it; we should be focused on the problems that are causing the behavior and solving them." If a child is not developing smoothly, then something is getting in the way. "Every kid has their own developmental trajectory. Every kid is doing as well as they possibly can at that point in development," he said.[110]

As parents, we often turn to tips and tricks when our kids are not meeting our expectations, offering them stickers or consequences as we insist harder. This is a missed opportunity to uncover what's really going on, to help our kids practice communicating about difficult topics, and to teach our kids how to solve problems. In contrast, Sigh, See, Start encourages us toward leadership by modeling how to approach problems through engaging meaningfully to find real solutions.

Collaboration and Parental Authority

Some parents find it hard to believe that collaborating with our children is good leadership. But the truth is, we are collaborating with them more than we think. Children are skilled and persistent negotiators with their playmates and parents, according to one study.[111] One survey of two thousand parents found that parents negotiate with their children six times a day on average, usually for about eight minutes each time. That means we spend about twenty-four hours a month, more or less, negotiating with our children, whether we like it or not.[112] Contrary to what many parents have been taught, negotiating with our children actually increases their sense of our authority. As Terri R. Kurtzberg writes in an article from Harvard's Program on Negotiation, children actually tune us out when parents use "because I said so." Instead, she writes, "You'll end up with much stronger compliance if you take your child's perspective into account and gain their buy-in."[113]

When we work with our children rather than dictating terms in a way they perceive as arbitrary, we show confident leadership and teach them a process for solving problems.[114] Nevertheless, sometimes we have to tell our kids that what they want is one of our nonnegotiables. This is a time when parents might say something like, "We've shared our perspectives with each other and I know we disagree, but as your parent I have to maintain this rule."

Collaborative and Proactive Solutions

My favorite tool for parents who want to get to the root of problems and work with their kids is Ross Greene's Collaborative and Proactive Solutions (CPS) model, which is a great example of how to supplement Sigh, See, Start in specific problem-solving situations. I first came across Greene's book *The Explosive Child: A New Approach for Understanding and Parenting Easily Frustrated, Chronically Inflexible Children* when my son was four years old. Well-behaved at school and daycare, my son had started having occasional but impressive tantrums at home when he was two. As a pediatrician, I trusted that he would outgrow them and I waited as patiently as I could. But by the time he was four his meltdowns at home were lasting forty-five to sixty minutes a couple of times a day. I assumed he was letting out the stress he'd been holding in all day at school—we had moved recently and he was getting used to a new home and new school. One day, after countless times when co-regulation had failed and I scooped up a screaming child and carried him to his car seat because we just had to get out the door, I picked up Greene's book. The subtitle and the first few pages described my son perfectly: great at school and explosive at home.

CPS teaches parents to collaborate with their child and solve problems proactively. Rather than reacting in the moment, when a parent is concerned about a child's behavior, they need to recognize that they are looking at an unsolved problem involving an expectation the child is having difficulty meeting. One clue that an expectation might not be working can show up in our behavior as parents: if we are routinely impatient, frustrated, or snapping at our kids in a certain scenario, that's a sign of an unsolved problem. To solve the problem, CPS offers three steps: express empathy by asking your child why meeting the expectation is hard for them; define adult expectations when you clarify why this particular expectation is important; and the invitation, when parent and child collaborate on a solution.

Sigh, See, Start enhances our ability to use other parenting techniques without turning them into rigid shoulds, and learning to use CPS is no exception. In this case, the steps dovetail beautifully. Because the first step in CPS is empathy, it helps to sigh in order to self-regulate before you start asking your child questions. Since the problem you want to address is one that upsets your child, it's important to communicate safety, genuine curiosity, and compassion to your child. Rather than asking pointless questions that put kids on the defensive—like "Why did you do that?"—gently gather information from your child about what's making it hard for them to meet a particular expectation. If they are hesitant, explain to your child that you are trying something new: solving problems together instead of simply telling them what to do. Greene's books are full of sample scripts to get a reluctant child talking.

When I tried this with my four-year-old, I took him out for a Frosty at Wendy's, because I felt a change of scenery would help him trust that we were going to do something different. I used some of the phrases Greene's book suggested and targeted a single problem: "I notice at bedtime you're having a hard time going to bed when you are supposed to and screaming a lot. What's up with that?" My son looked at me suspiciously, having never been invited to share his perspective like this. He was so little: all he'd known from his parents and teachers was being told how things were. It took several minutes to convince him that I was truly interested in what he thought before he told me what was going on. Apparently, my son did not like sharing a room with his two-year-old brother, who would try to wrestle when he was falling asleep.

Next, remember to see mindfully when you move to step two in CPS. Define adult expectations, and ask yourself why a particular expectation is important. Why do I have this expectation for this child? Why is it important that this expectation be met? Is it a good one for us? An expectation is important depending on how the unsolved problem is affecting the child or how it is affecting other people. Important issues are usually ones of health, safety, or learning. On the other hand, if you don't know why you have the expectation or it has to do with other people's opinions, then drop it.

Finally, start approaching problems in a new way when you reach the third step in CPS, the invitation. This is when a parent and child collaborate on a solution. The proposed solution has to be realistic and mutually satisfactory or it won't work. "Both parties have to be able to do what they're agreeing to, and the solution has to address the concerns of both parties," said Greene. If the solution only addresses the concern of the adult, then the child's concern has not been heard. The child will feel that they do not have a voice, leaving them feeling angry or helpless. On the other hand, if the solution only addresses the concerns of the child, the parents have silenced their own voice. Without a voice, parents cannot have the influence they need to provide good leadership to their children.[115]

That day at Wendy's I again used a script from Greene's book, "Wow! Having your brother jumping on you when you are trying to sleep sounds terrible. I would hate that, too. I was hoping we could share what's important to each of us and try to find something that would work better." After that, I explained that his father and I felt going to bed on time was very important so he could be healthy and feel happy. My son shared that not only did he want to be able to fall asleep without being jumped on, but that he wanted some alone time and more time to color. I felt so embarrassed. How could I have missed that my born introvert was spending all day with other kids at daycare, and then the rest of his time with his noisy extroverted little brother? Of course he was overwhelmed. Eventually, we hit on the idea that we would put his little brother down to bed thirty minutes before him so that he would be asleep by the time my older son went to bed. During that time, my son would color by himself at his art table in the basement and everyone, including Mom and Dad, would leave him alone.

My son astonished me with his strengths: he was able to identify a need, solve a problem, and negotiate in a surprisingly mature way with an adult. In the quote he is most known for, Greene says, "Kids do well when they can do well," a lesson I never forget. We began the new bedtime routine that very night. Not only did my son go to bed easily, but over the next few days his meltdowns at other times disappeared, too. With his stress around bedtime removed, he had more energy to self-regulate throughout the day.

In another example, Liam found making his bed overwhelming because his bed was covered with stuffed animals. Yet making his bed every day was one of his mother's expectations. His solution? "I just sleep on top of the covers and so I don't have to make it in the morning," Liam told me. "And that means less work for me in the morning, besides getting dressed. My grandma said my mom did exactly the same thing when she was a kid." In this way Liam was able to meet his mother's expectation in a way that worked for both of them.

Liam's story is a great example of why the solutions we collaborate with our kids on are so individual. This solution might not be practical in every family, due to allergies or other issues. In another family you might choose to leave the bed unmade or move the stuffed animals to another location.

Coaching Our Kids to Help Them Meet Expectations

Once we've collaborated with our kids on our expectations, our job as parents is to coach our kids on their way to reaching those goals. My college fencing coach had a magic formula: He believed in my ability more than I did. He taught me the specific skills I needed, and he encouraged me to adopt a fencing style that worked for me, even when it was very different from that of my teammates. Coaching like this is the opposite of over-nurturing; instead of swooping in to do things for our kids, great coaches support their athletes to face their own challenges and grow in the process.

When it comes to offering kids support, the Yale Child Study Center has found that a specific formula works best. In this case, support means making a statement that communicates both validation for the child's feelings and confidence in the child's ability. So support = acceptance validation + confidence. In order to both accept what the child is feeling and validate it, parents can say something empathetic like, "I see that this is hard for you," or "You've always been a worrier." A lot of us stop there, not realizing that we may have communicated sympathy, but we've also reinforced the child's anxiety. On the other hand, statements that communicate confidence include, "I am 100 percent sure that you can handle it," "You're fine," or even "You just have to power through it." These comments express the parent's belief in the child's ability, but they also ignore the child's feelings and leave them feeling invisible and alone with their anxiety. It is only when we combine validation with confidence that we communicate true support: "I see that this is hard for you and I am 100 percent sure that you can handle it," or "Anxiety is uncomfortable, but I am sure that you can cope!"[116]

Sometimes, no matter how much support we offer, we discover that our child simply doesn't have the skills to meet an expectation we have determined to be reasonable and important. That's when we need to consider the possibility of developmental differences. This can be an important time to meet with your child's pediatrician to discuss what you are seeing. Depending on their age and behaviors, evaluations for developmental or learning delays, sensory processing difficulties, ADHD, autism spectrum disorder, and others may be appropriate. For example, babies with sensory processing difficulties may present with extreme colic that does not respond to the usual treatment. Later, a child with sensory processing difficulties may have tantrums because they are constantly overwhelmed by the world's sensory input and operating in fight-or-flight. Or a child who is described as oppositional, defiant, lazy, and irresponsible may actually have undiagnosed ADHD and be unable to keep track of time, organize themselves to do tasks, or manage labile emotions. If you suspect this might be the case, work with your pediatrician; they may be able to recommend tools to help you, including pediatric occupational therapy.

Don't fall for the assumption that if a child can meet an expectation sometimes, then they can meet it all the time (or that failure to meet expectations means laziness or lack of motivation). Kids with developmental delays or neuro-atypical brains are working so much harder than other kids all day long to meet expectations, and sometimes they simply cannot do what they manage at other times. This is why families who are raising kids with developmental differences benefit so much from the support of therapies that help kids develop the skills they don't have. Finding the time or financial wherewithal to access those therapies can be a challenge for parents, but they make a big difference for kids.[117]

Scaffolding

If we uncover a weak spot in a child's skillset or a developmental delay, we can use an approach called scaffolding, a term that comes from the process of constructing a new building. As parts of the building are completed, the scaffolding is gradually removed. Scaffolding in child development refers to the way a caregiver offers just enough support for the child to accomplish a task by themselves. Every parent does this with very young children when we offer them our fingers to grab onto while they are learning to walk, or when we encourage them to get back up when they fall. Most of the time we offer considerably less scaffolding as our children get older, but kids with developmental challenges continue to need it.

Sigh, See, Start helps us provide the right amount of scaffolding for our child. Imagine a child with executive function difficulties who is freaking out at homework time. As the parent sighs to keep themself calm, they may see their child's obvious distress in the moment, while mentally seeing what they have learned about how their child's ADHD makes getting started on a task overwhelming. Then they may start by co-regulating with their child, saying, "I'm here. It's okay. We'll take a look together," and perhaps rubbing their child's back. Once the child is calmer they might try collaborating (which can be a form of scaffolding) by asking their child, "What's going on?" Perhaps their child says that they don't know where to start or it's all too much, or perhaps they say, "I don't know." The parent might respond, "Last week when you felt this way about homework it was because it felt like too much and you were having trouble figuring out how to get started. I wonder if that might be going on today?" And then, when the child gives a moan of assent, the parent says, "Okay, let's look at your homework assignment list and break it down into smaller pieces." After practicing this together, the parent can reinforce their child's learning by offering support: "You know, ADHD makes it hard to break down a problem, especially when you're having big feelings, but the more we practice calming down and making a homework plan, the more you'll be able to do it yourself. And I'm so proud of you because you found a way that worked for you today and did the homework even though it felt hard."

Scaffolding is entirely different from the over-nurturing or pushing of intensive parenting: it doesn't do things for the child, nor does it leave the child alone without support to just push through. It always emphasizes building the child's skills and empowering the child to do things themselves, but never shames them for needing support along the way.

Sometimes Leadership Means Getting Outside Help

As I said earlier in the book, if we aren't making progress with behavioral concerns, or mental health is a concern, seeing a therapist or pediatrician is our first line of defense. When kids develop true anxiety disorders, or are dealing with depression, parents cannot handle it alone—no one can. I think part of what makes some parents hesitate to seek help from a pediatrician or a therapist is that parenting culture has told them these problems are their fault. Here's where research can bring parents comfort, because studies show that when kids have true anxiety disorders, parenting is not the cause. Rather, parents of anxious children adapt their behaviors to those children. Their loving attempts to help their children with overwhelming anxiety may look like coddling from the outside, but it's part of a natural response.

What we are talking about here is different from the consequences of the harmful parenting practices we looked at earlier in the book. Yes, parents who abuse their kids or use corporal punishment or verbal shaming can cause PTSD or depression in their kids. Parents who let their own unmanaged anxiety drive them to invasive over-nurturing can disrupt their children's development and make their children feel anxious.

All parents are involved in their children's anxiety because anxiety is part of a social system. Eli Lebowitz of the Yale Child Study Center explains it this way: human adults, like all mammals, may handle a threat directly by fighting or fleeing, but our young, who are born vulnerable and unable to self-soothe, respond to threats by sending social signals of distress to their caregivers. This system is hardwired, which means that all parents are deeply involved in their children's healthy anxiety systems. And that's a good thing: as we've learned in prior chapters, this caregiver response system, i.e., co-regulation, is the foundation for a child's development of secure attachment and eventual self-regulation.

In the case of a child with an unhealthy anxiety disorder, where the child's anxiety system is chronically activated, parents develop a behavioral pattern Lebowitz calls "family accommodation." These loving parents change their own behaviors in all sorts of ways to avoid triggering their child's anxiety, or to soothe it once triggered. For example, a parent might constantly arrive at work late in order to reduce their child's separation anxiety. Another parent might drive a special route to avoid going over bridges due to their child's fear of heights. Other families observe rigid schedules because change provokes higher anxiety in a child. Such family accommodation is present in 95 percent of parents with an anxious child. Unfortunately, accommodations may soothe a child in the moment, but they actually reinforce the child's anxiety over time by showing the child that they can't handle things themselves.

Parents in this situation often receive a lot of unfair criticism from outside observers, who blame them for making their child anxious, rather than understanding that parents are doing the best they can to help their child and responding to their own brain's hard-wired caregiving system. Such observers have no idea how exhausted and trapped such parents feel, nor have they seen the alarming levels of distress a child can show when parents don't accommodate them. This is a situation that parents cannot handle alone, and working with a good therapist can be invaluable. Lebowitz's book, *Breaking Free of Childhood Anxiety and OCD*, is a great resource for parents.[118]

* * *

Sigh, See, Start is all about being with our kids as they are and working with them where they are. When kids have parents who provide this kind of leadership, they feel more secure and supported in reaching their goals. But not everything in parenting is about solving problems. In the next chapter, we'll finally get to have some fun, as we explore how playing with our kids can operate as a valuable tool for family development.

CHAPTER 8 : KEY TAKEAWAYS

- Kids need good leadership, which involves setting expectations, coaching our kids to reach them, and cheering them on.
- Undesirable behavior happens when a child is unable to meet an expectation.
- Collaborative problem-solving helps a child develop their own skills and voice.
- Supporting a child means offering both validation and confidence.
- Scaffolding means supporting a child where they are weak until they gradually build skills.
- Praise effort, not outcomes, to build genuine confidence.
- Family meetings provide a structured setting to practice Sigh, See, Start.

Chapter 9

The Power of Play

Play is not frivolous. It is not something to do after the "real work" is done. Play is the real work of childhood. Through it, children have their best chance for becoming whole, happy adults.

—Bright Horizons, "The Benefits of Play for a Child's Development"

Play—for children and adults—seems to be one of the first casualties of the ShouldStorm's focus on achievement at all costs. This may not come as a surprise, as the importance of play and the negative consequences of cutting school recess and outdoor neighborhood playtime are well documented.[119] But even though the United Nations Commission on Human Rights has declared play a fundamental right of every child,[120] the imperative to keep our children safe and focus on maximizing their effort in ever increasing hours of homework and organized activities feels more urgent than the need to give kids space to "waste time" with free play.[121]

And yet, play is central to what it means to be a social creature, and not just in human children or even in mammals: scientists have recently discovered that even frogs, fish, lizards, and bees play.[122] By definition, play is something done for its own sake, for no purpose other than enjoyment of the activity. Psychiatrist Stuart Brown writes, "It's voluntary, it's pleasurable, it offers a sense of engagement, it takes you out of time. And the act itself is more important than the outcome."[123] Experts believe this spontaneity helps the young develop valuable skills they can obtain no other way. Why, then, are we allowing our culture to rob our children of this irreplaceable opportunity?

Restoring play as central to our families can help to counteract anxiety, support the social and emotional growth of our children, increase resilience, and build their creative problem-solving skills. Play bonds a family together, helping us grow individually and as a group. And because our kids learn best if we learn together, play helps families practice recognizing mistakes as opportunities.

Sigh, See, Start is about being with our kids as they are and supporting them in who they are becoming. Play is when kids show us these aspects of themselves. Engaging with and enjoying our kids during play helps us create the relationship we want with our children. Because play is a time when we put the worries of the world aside, let down our guard, and have fun, it can forge powerful connections.

There are several different ways of relating to our kids during play, and each has value.

Child-Centered Play

Taking the lead is so natural to parents that we don't even realize how often we exert our authority over our kids. We know good leadership is essential, but something wonderful happens when we occasionally let go of the reins. This is called child-centered or nondirective play, which means that you set aside a time and place when your child can take the lead, while you give them your full attention, describing what they are doing with appreciation.

For parents, following their child's lead is harder than we realize. Think of the last time you sat down to play one-on-one with your child. How long did it take before you started making suggestions? During child-centered play the child is in charge; the child leads and we follow. As we attune to our child and show our enthusiasm for what they are doing, we are showing love and acceptance for their deepest self and our children learn they can trust us with their inner-most thoughts—because that is what their play is communicating.

Researchers have found that regularly engaging in nondirective play with our children has multiple benefits: it strengthens the parent-child bond, reduces the child's anxiety level in general, improves the child's social skills, and helps parents take a more positive and encouraging approach to the child throughout the day.[124] Fortunately, researchers have also found that we can have this transformative impact in only five minutes a day, when done regularly.[125] Because during child-centered play we intentionally shift our usual dynamic by allowing our child to feel in control while we pay attention to positive behaviors, we'll find that the parenting skills we learn and the more relaxed tone in our parent-child relationship carry over into other parts of the day.[126]

When my children were in early elementary school, my husband and I used the five minutes a day child-directed play method from psychologist Donna Pincus's book *Growing Up Brave*, and it was every bit as helpful as the research predicted. The whole routine took a total of fifteen minutes a day, including setting up and gathering the kids, as each parent spent five minutes one-on-one with each of our two children. Following her instructions, we set aside a "daily special time" box of toys for each boy, full of Play-Doh, Legos and other building toys, art supplies, and a playset with townspeople. We also heeded Pincus's warning to avoid toys for battle play, board games, or anything involving competition. Because we clearly differentiated

CHILD-CENTERED PLAY with
SIGH, SEE, START

SIGH

Let go of everything else but this time with your child.
Put aside worries, your to-do list, and time pressure
and set the timer for five minutes, knowing that your to-do
list can wait that long.

SEE

Turn your full attention to this moment with your child
and to what they are doing. Draw on a sense
of appreciation for them and their play. Tune into your
child's state of energy and mood.

START

Follow their lead and start imitating them or doing
what they tell you to do. Use "I notice" statements
to describe their art or their play with a positive tone of
voice. Attune to your child by matching their level of
energy and enthusiasm. (Matching them helps you avoid
overdoing it and weirding them out by hovering.)

the time as special and distinct from what we normally did, our kids knew when they got to be in charge.[127]

By putting the child in control, child-centered play helps build their confidence in themselves and in their parents' appreciation for their ideas. If we do anything to interfere with that control we are, in essence, shutting them down and telling them that what they are showing us is not good enough. That means we absolutely have to avoid taking over in the subtle ways parents do, such as bugging them with directive questions like, "Should the horse go in the barn?" or "Doesn't that Lego go there?" Instead, our job is to imitate what our kids are doing, and to offer them reflective listening with the type of praise we discussed in the last chapter. If your child describes what they are doing, reflect it back to them by describing what they are doing in positive terms.[128]

* * *

When our children invite us into their inner world by showing us their play, we have a special opportunity to honor their inner life by showing our respect, enthusiasm, and attention for their imagination. We are giving them a gift of love that we can give no other way. To be seen and appreciated in the center of who we are is a transformative experience, and one we all need, especially from our parents.

Many parents feel pressure to do all the fun things as a family, not realizing that one-on-one time is magical. On weekends, when the family is together from Friday evening to Monday morning, Andrew and Eitan have learned to "divide and conquer." Andrew reflected, "The kids are so amazing when they're not together. It's so different when they're apart. They can both be so well behaved if they have just the focus of one parent." When siblings are together, they inevitably compete for our attention, but when we eliminate that rivalry during one-on-one time, we give our kids space to relax and enjoy their time with us.

By the time our kids reach the preteen years, they find child-centered play time embarrassing, but we can still apply the same child-centered principles and set aside special time with them. (Just don't call it "special time" or you might get an eye roll or be told, "Mom, you are so cringe," as I have been.) The further they move into adolescence, the more likely kids are to favor spontaneous moments of communication. If your adolescent pops in to tell you about something funny a friend did at lunch or the project they are working on for school or wants to play their instrument for you right now, drop everything when possible and give them your full attention. These are moments when they are offering us their inner world and hoping for our warmth and appreciation. Because adolescents are at such an awkward stage of their social development, they tend to shut down if we put them off until later.

Of course, it also helps to set aside times when spontaneous communication is likely to happen with an adolescent. Car rides are well-known as a time when kids tend to talk with us, perhaps because they don't have to face the intensity of our eye contact. We've found the same is true when we walk the dogs together; it's a time when my quieter son will predictably start talking. The same son has often told me how much he values the weekly times we sit next to each other in the car and eat ice cream, just the two of us. Shared experiences like going on a roller coaster together also tend to open things up, but that is usually not an everyday occurrence, and the goal is to build in as many regular opportunities as possible.

Experts will tell you not to use electronics, but sometimes we have to make the best of the situation we are in. In times of illness, I've had to find stationary ways to connect with my sons that don't take a lot of mental effort—so these days we connect by watching shows together. Most often, I keep it child-centered by letting them pick what we watch during our daily thirty minutes of one-on-one time. Sometimes it's a TV show with a great storyline that we enjoy together and chat about. Other times we watch comedy, laughing together and making jokes. My kids know it's the best I can do right now, and it's still a moment to show them I appreciate who they are and what they find interesting.

Parent-Coached Play

Whenever we are not paying the extraordinary attention it takes to make space for child-centered play, parents automatically start coaching our kids. And that's just fine, because when we keep the child at the center, taking on that natural coaching role is a good thing. If we can avoid hovering and let kids stay in control of their play, we will find ample opportunity to advise our children on aspirations (go for it, climb higher, you can do it), safety (please don't climb there), emotional regulation (I know you are disappointed and I also know you can get up and try again), social skills (I see another kid your age over there—why don't you see if they want to play?), and conflict resolution with other children. If we use Sigh, See, Start to tune into our children's state in these moments, our coaching has more impact than it might at other times because we are engaging our children in something they care about at the moment.

Al takes his role as a coach for his daughters very seriously, and he loves it. "I let them lead me to what they are looking to play with and I meet them at their level," he told me. When the girls build forts out of the cushions in the basement, Al challenges them to think. "I try to explain to them the engineering side of why that didn't work. We started talking about why you need support here if you are going to put your body on this. I originally viewed this as being the fun dad. But it's so much more than that. It brings us closer and our relationship is stronger because we can go back and forth and collaborate on ideas about how to play," said Al. One time, two-and-a-half-year-old Gracie asked "Dad, how do we become real princesses?" Al jumped on the opportunity to impart some of his values. "A real princess can do a lot," said Al. "They're very smart. They're very kind. But they're also really good at obstacle courses, and they're good at helping each other." Gracie wanted to know more, so Al set up an obstacle course and then told his daughters, "You can only be a princess if both of you complete the obstacle course and you do it the right way, without my help." The girls ran the course a few times, communicating with each other and working together until they were able to succeed at each obstacle without Al's help. Al noticed four-and-a-half-year-old Natalie was imitating him at times, taking on a coaching role herself, even as she accepted Gracie's efforts to correct her when she got something wrong. At the end, they held a celebration and the girls declared themselves real princesses. "That was probably my proudest moment as a dad so far. I felt like they were going to use this one day."

Of course, coaching doesn't always go this smoothly. When Al coached Gracie's soccer team, his daughter spent the entire first practice laying in the middle of the field, because she just didn't want to play soccer. "It was so embarrassing, and I had to tell the parents that it was okay because she was mine," said Al. Gracie eventually came around and declared she loved soccer, only for Al to learn it was because of the snacks.

Play as a Family

A common saying goes, "The family that plays together stays together," but I would rephrase that as, "The family that plays together grows together." When we play, we show a unique side of ourselves, as we delve into fun and enjoyment and let go of our self-consciousness. Adults known for their gravitas are suddenly joyfully and wildly silly. Thus, we give each other a gift of intimacy, of knowing and being known. And when we enter into this playful state, we also show our children how delighted we are by them, in a way we simply can't at more serious times. The Sigh, See, Start perspective recognizes that families are made up of different individuals at different stages of maturity who are all growing together. When that family plays together, it enhances that growth.

"Kids have a real sense of wonder and curiosity that seems unfiltered and raw," said Eitan. When he plays with his kids in a way that lets him see through their eyes, he feels like they get in sync with each other in a special way.

Research shows that family play boosts wellbeing in both children and their parents.[129] Experiments in family play also found that the nonthreatening and engaging nature of play allowed everyone to practice their problem-solving skills and led to significant improvements in family relations.[130]

But what kind of play brings these kinds of benefits as a family? In my opinion, play that emphasizes imagination and collaboration among family members builds the relationship far better than games that set us in direct competition (or conflict) with each other, such as Monopoly or Sorry. Collaborative games in which all the players work together to compete against the game are a favorite in my house. In one of the first we played, Mole Rats in Space, we, the mole rats, had to collect our equipment and escape from our space station before invading snakes bit us. As the kids got older we enjoyed similar games like Forbidden Island and Pandemic, one of the original collaborative games in which participants play as the Centers for Disease Control trying to contain a disease outbreak. Because these games involve competition, they bring up big feelings of excitement and frustration, but because we are not competing against each other, we can practice emotional regulation with minimal bickering.

When play adds imagination to collaboration, we take the family bonding in play to the next level. Tabletop roleplaying games like No Thank You Evil are wonderful for elementary school-age kids. In this game, players create their own characters and then set out on adventures led by their guide, usually a parent. They work together to overcome obstacles in adorable settings like Dragonsnot Falls and Whizbang's broken time machine. Because the players get to act out their characters and create their own dialogue, family members get to see themselves and each other in a new way. As kids get older, families can graduate to similar games like Dungeons and Dragons, which provides similar imaginative play for adolescents and adults.

Free play is also great for families, and can take the form of playing catch, hide-and-seek, or tag on the playground. In addition, going for hikes, playing at the beach or the pool, or going on family bike rides can also be forms of play, as long as everyone enjoys them. Such moments can act as a reset button: when Monique finds her family is growing grumpy, she takes them out for a walk or a bike ride. She also sets aside family Fridays as a regular chance for everyone to play together. Video games also have their place in family play: lots of parents tell me about the joy they share when they play a rousing game of Mario Kart with their kids. If it's fun and we get to be ourselves, then it's valuable as play.

Play as Parenting

Recently a method called playful parenting has been popular, and it offers some great tools. But like so many things, when we filter it through the ShouldStorm, we can take it too far, to an inauthentic place that's not helpful for our kids.

We can all recognize the value of a playful approach to our kids, as we learned from Mary Poppins motivating the children to clean up while singing, "In every job that's to be done, there is an element of fun." A few years ago, Eitan felt inspired by a book about playful parenting, which taught him both to engage with his children through play and to use play as a behavior management technique.

The playful approach gave Eitan tools to use with his six-year-old daughter, who has some developmental challenges and becomes dysregulated easily. "For example, she doesn't want to brush her teeth. She's so distracted and so unfocused that she doesn't even hear me when I'm saying, 'Brush your teeth.' She's just focusing on the shiny object," Eitan explained. "And there are a couple of ways to get her to be more compliant. I will get down on my knees to become a unicorn, and I will offer a unicorn ride to the bathroom. That works. She hops on my back. Or sometimes she pretends she's a kitten or a puppy and I'll say, 'Here kitty,' and she crawls right over to the bathroom. I say, 'Kitty, use your toothbrush. You know you are cutting your teeth.'"

All of that sounds reasonable, but Eitan worried me when he referred to play as a way to get compliance, a feature of several popular behavioral management methods that use play. If play is something we do simply for the joy of it, then using it as a tool to gain compliance takes the heart right out of it. It might help us in the short term with getting our kids to do what we want them to in the moment, but we may miss out on the much greater relationship growth we've been talking about in this chapter. When we use play for an agenda, it stops being play and our children may eventually see us as manipulative and insincere.

Here's where Sigh, See, Start can help us make choices about how to apply parenting advice in a way that meets our child's genuine needs. We know that we need to keep the child at the center of play and let them take the lead, without turning play into a way to manage them. What Eitan actually did in action was to tune into his child's state and what she was interested in and then offer that to her in a very Mary Poppins–like way. His playful approach met her at her level and allowed him to co-regulate with her when she was dysregulated about a task she disliked. Even though he talked about getting compliance, in action Eitan was using the tool appropriately, by supporting and co-regulating with his child.

Eitan also recognizes that playful parenting cannot be a one-size-fits-all solution. He's seen other parents take it too far, as they try to apply the same playful method to every situation. "I have a good friend who really lives that ethos. Her son will say, 'Hey, I have a great idea. Why don't you wake me up at 2:00 a.m. and we'll have a slumber party in the tent in my room?' and she does it," even though disrupting sleep in kids has a negative impact on their wellbeing and development. With Sigh, See, Start, we can mindfully take what we find helpful from parenting advice, add it to our toolkit, and use it when it works for us.

Free Play (Alone or Together)

In addition to play with their parents or as a family, kids need time to play freely, without adults around. Kids who have enough open-ended, unscheduled times in their lives to just play are happier and more resilient to stress. During free play, kids don't have to worry about what adults think; they get a chance to express whatever thoughts and feelings they are exploring right then. This is what distinguishes free play from structured play, such as a sports team or an art class with expectations enforced by an adult, or a video game with rules and parameters set by the game designer.

Free play has a tremendous impact on every aspect of child development: creativity, cognitive and emotional skills, decision-making skills, and physical dexterity and strength. They "move at their own pace, discover their own areas of interest, and ultimately engage fully in the passions they wish to pursue," according to research by the American Academy of Pediatrics. To a child, the world is very big and run by big people, but in play a child creates and explores a world they can master, facing and even conquering their fears.[131]

Alone, children spend time with themselves, expressing who they are becoming and growing more comfortable in who they are.

Individual free play is a key time when children form a sense of their own identity, as well as likes, dislikes, and even passions. Not infrequently, whatever a child is really into at around age ten or eleven years old forms the basis of their future passion in life.

An important way to enhance your child's free play is to provide a rich play environment, full of different materials. Dirt, sand, sticks, blocks, clay, Play-Doh, and water tables are wonderful materials for play. Dolls and dollhouses, action figures, and playsets are also lots of fun. It's helpful to plan time for your children without screens or structure, so they have time for this kind of free play. I often tell families that if your child doesn't have time to get bored, they are overscheduled, because it is when kids are bored that they engage their creativity and engage in play.

When children play freely together, they engage their imaginations together and build social skills in the process. Often, they practice adult roles, decision-making, sharing, self-advocacy skills, and even conflict resolution.[132] In one study, researchers found that children as young as two and three years old were skilled negotiators during play. The children would agree about their play and then use different strategies to change those agreements as they went along. The study authors noted that these negotiations, which were a central part of the children's play, had a "clear purpose: to agree on both how they can be together in their play and the content of their play."[133]

Play also helps kids make sense of their world. During the COVID-19 pandemic, researchers observed children in daycare in both Finland and Sweden and found they used play, humor, and creativity as coping tools. In particular, the children invented games like "being at the hospital" and "corona tag" to face their fears of spreading or catching the infection. They also made up coronavirus-related songs, rhymes, and drawings—all forms of play that helped them sort out their experiences.[134]

Play and Challenge

One element of children's free play that worries parents, especially when children are in groups, is the way play naturally drives kids to challenge themselves, finding out how much they can do and what their limits are. Because there is an inherent risk of injury when kids do this physically, parents are appropriately wary. But while in past generations a certain amount of injury was accepted as part of childhood, in our current culture keeping our children perfectly safe has become an unhealthy imperative for parents. When I was a kid, the teachers, school nurses, and parents didn't worry at all about all of my skinned knees from recess on the playground, but these days I've seen parents carry surprising levels of guilt about their children's shins being mildly bruised from banging them during healthy play. We need to give ourselves a break and give our kids room to learn what their bodies are urging them to learn through play.

Children naturally create risk in their play, which allows them to build essential skills they need later in life. Think of learning to ride a bike: if we don't take the risk of trying to go without training wheels, we never accomplish our goal, but if we take too great a risk before we are ready, we crash. Research literature from multiple disciplines has shown that our culture's goal of keeping kids as safe as possible interferes with healthy child development. Researchers recommend that instead we change our focus to keeping children no safer than necessary while still allowing some risky play outdoors, so we can better meet their needs.[135]

Sigh, See, Start helps us decide what risks are worthwhile for our kids. When you sigh and then see your child, you can assess whether their skills match what they are about to try. Then start encouraging them as you feel appropriate.

There are a few things more antithetical to the ShouldStorm than play. Letting go of our worries and entering into joy together is at the heart of what it means to be a family. It is during play that our eyes sparkle with the joy of being alive, that our curiosity shines through, and that we learn to trust each other effortlessly.

CHAPTER 9 : KEY TAKEAWAYS

- Play is something we do for its own sake, just for the fun of it.
- When children play, they are developing essential developmental skills.
- Child-centered play means that the child leads and the parent gives their full attention and appreciation.
- When parents engage children in their play, they boost family wellbeing and resilience.

Expanding Your Toolkit

n this book you've learned that what your child needs most is you—your engagement and your genuine presence. When you use Sigh, See, Start, you tune into your child and you tune out the culture of criticism. Often Sigh, See, Start is enough, and for times when you need more specific tools, I've offered a number of approaches that complement Sigh, See, Start in Part 3 of this book.

But what happens when you come up against a situation this book has not addressed? Or you hear about a really great parenting method you'd like to try? You can apply your Sigh, See, Start mindset fearlessly to evaluate whether that parenting advice is something you want to add to your toolkit or not.

When you want to decide if parenting advice is right for your family, consider the following criteria:

1. Does this method employ mindful acceptance of how things are? Is it compassionate to parent and child?
2. Is this method strength-based? Does it believe in the ability of parent and child to handle challenges?
3. Is it developmental? Does it support a child progressively building skills starting at their current level?
4. Is it non-shaming? Does it accept parents and kids where they are right now and gently bring them along?
5. Does it have realistic goals? Is it non-perfectionistic?

Sigh, See, Start can enhance a parent's ability to apply any parenting advice, but I encourage you to expand your toolbox only with methods that meet the above criteria.

APPENDIX

SIGH, SEE, START WORKSHEET

Use this worksheet to break down tricky problems
with Sigh, See, Start.

What is the problem, worry, or challenge you are facing?

SIGH

How do you feel about this?

_____

What are the shoulds that come up for you?

_____

Who are you blaming (yourself or others) for not living up to
those shoulds?

_____

How much time and energy, physical or emotional, do you have
to tackle this?

_____

_____

_____

SEE

Can you clarify the nature of the problem?

_____

Who is involved?

_____

What have they told you? What do their behaviors tell you?

_____

_____

Who is upset by this?

_____

Are multiple individuals influencing each other?

_____

_____

What else do you observe?

_____

_____

START

Take stock of what you have learned about this issue and your realistic resources to address it.

_____

_____

_____

_____

How important is this problem right now? Is there another one that needs to take priority?

_____

_____

_____

_____

GENERATE POSSIBLE TACTICS TO TRY FOR SOLVING THE PROBLEM, SUCH AS:

→ Try something your child has already suggested.

→ Practice co-regulation.

→ Engage in one-on-one play with your child.

→ Hold a collaborative problem-solving session with your child or children (or your partner if you have a baby).

→ Seek outside support, such as from your pediatrician or therapist.

ACKNOWLEDGMENTS

As a pediatrician, my most important teachers are the parents and children who have generously shared their lives with me. Any true wisdom in this book comes from what they have taught me through their love for each other, their hopes, their fears, their challenges, and their victories. In particular, those parents and kids who told their personal stories in interviews for this book gave a tremendous gift.

Makeba Rasin is a brilliant editor, a beautiful writer, and an amazing human being. She grappled with the ideas, pushed me to the next level as a writer, and joined me in using Sigh, See, Start with our kids. Without her this book would be twice as wordy and half as clear.

My agent, Laurie Liss, did more than advocate for this book; she was the first to show me that Sigh, See, Start was not simply a method, but a mindset. She went the extra mile when she acted as an editor and a mentor, insisting I trust my voice.

When I was still wondering whether the world needed another parenting book, I met Sam Horn. Fifteen minutes later she had convinced me I had a moral obligation to write this book, workshopped the title, coached me on giving a TEDx talk, and begun making introductions.

At PA Press, Jennifer Thompson has been an engaged editor, a compassionate human, and a parent who showed me Sigh, See, Start's value by using it with her own child. Working with her has been a complete pleasure.

Hara Marano, my editor at *Psychology Today*, has mentored me by talking through my ideas and walking me through writing a book proposal. Members of my writers' group at The Mentor Project are an endless source of encouragement, not to mention full of exciting ideas of their own. The team at TEDxNaperville gave me the opportunity to bring the ideas in this book to the public and have a great time doing it. Thanks to all of my colleagues, friends, and neighbors who have encouraged me to write this book.

So many experts in their fields generously shared their time and knowledge with me. Caitlyn Collins, Ross Greene, Stephen Porges, Deb Dana, Tina Payne Bryson, Richard Schwartz, Frank Anderson, and Moran Cerf deepened my thinking in countless ways and provided valuable interview material for this book.

Everything I know about being a mother I have learned from my sons, Miles and Connor. Your endless curiosity and creativity make being your mother so much fun, and your kind hearts are all a mother could wish for.

And most of all, thanks to my husband for the editing help, believing in me even at the times when I have doubted myself, and for putting up with the times when I was hyper-focused on writing and oblivious to the world around me. You are a wonderful, dedicated father, and my best friend.

NOTES

Introduction

1   Jessica Winter, "The Harsh Realm of 'Gentle Parenting,'" *New Yorker*, March 23, 2022, www.newyorker.com/books/under-review/the-harsh-realm-of-gentle-parenting.

2   Patrick Ishizuka, "Social Class, Gender, and Contemporary Parenting Standards in the United States: Evidence from a National Survey Experiment," *Social Forces* 98, no. 1 (September 2019): 31–58.

3   Caitlyn Collins, *Making Motherhood Work: How Women Manage Careers and Caregiving* (Princeton: Princeton University Press, 2019), 8.

4   Jennifer Senior, *All Joy, No Fun: The Paradox of Modern Parenting* (New York: Ecco, 2014), 55.

5   Collins, *Making Motherhood Work*, 199.

6   Monica Hesse, "The Unreasonable Expectations of American Motherhood," *Washington Post*, June 15, 2021, www.washingtonpost.com/lifestyle/style/birth-rate-american-mothers/2021/06/14/045c4684-c950-11eb-81b1-34796c7393af_story.html.

7   Robyn Koslowitz, "Parental Burnout: What Makes It Different," *Psychology Today*, July 9, 2020, www.psychologytoday.com/intl/blog/targeted-parenting/202007/parental-burnout-what-makes-it-different.

8   Moira Mikolajczak, "Is Parental Burnout Distinct from Job Burnout and Depressive Symptoms?" *Clinical Psychological Science* 8, no. 4 (July 2020): 673–89.

9   E. Z. Tronick and A. Gianino, "Interactive Mismatch and Repair: Challenges to the Coping Infant," *Zero to Three* 6, no. 3 (1986): 1–6.

10   Fred Rogers, *The World According to Mister Rogers: Important Things to Remember* (New York: Hachette Books, 2019).

Chapter 1

11   Alison Escalante, "Shame Works to Control Kids… and That's a Problem," *Psychology Today*, August 18, 2019, www.psychologytoday.com/intl/blog/shouldstorm/201908/shame-works-control-kids-and-s-problem.

12   Escalante, "Shame Works."

13   Annalisa Barbieri, "Jean Liedloff Obiturary," *Guardian*, April 11, 2011, www.theguardian.com/lifeandstyle/2011/apr/11/jean-liedloff-obituary.

14   "Understanding the Continuum Concept," Continuum Concept, accessed February 7, 2023, continuumconcept.org/summary.

15   Kate Pickert, "The Man Who Remade Motherhood," *Time*, May 21, 2012, time.com/606/the-man-who-remade-motherhood/.

16   Barbieri, "Jean Liedloff."

17   "FAQ," Attached at the Heart, accessed May 1, 2023, attachedattheheart.attachmentparenting.org/faq/.

18   William Sears, *Growing Together: A Parent's Guide to Baby's First Year* (Franklin Park, IL: La Leche League International, 1987).

19   Tronick and Gianino, "Interactive Mismatch," 1–6.

20   Pikert, "Man Who Remade Motherhood."

21   Kevin Giles, "Post-1970s Evangelical Responses to the Emancipation of Women," *Priscilla Papers: The Academic Journal of CBE International* 20, no. 4 (Fall 2006).

22   Pickert, "Man Who Remade Motherhood."

23   William and Martha Sears, *The Complete Book of Christian Parenting and Child Care* (Nashville: B&H Books, 1997).

24   Pickert, "Man Who Remade Motherhood."

25   Sears, *Growing Together.*

26   Saul McLeod, "Konrad Lorenz: Theory of Imprinting in Psychology," *Simply Psychology,* February 16, 2023, www.simplypsychology.org/konrad-lorenz.html.

27   Philip Guiton, "Early Experience and Sexual Object-Choice in the Brown Leghorn," *Animal Behavior* 14, no. 4 (October 1966): 534–38.

28   Sandra H. Klein, Howard S. Hoffman, and Peter DePaulo, "Some Effects of Early Social Stimulation on the Emotional Reactivity of Ducklings," *Animal Learning & Behavior* 4, no. 3 (September 1976): 257–60.

29   Saul Mcleod, "John Bowlby Attachment Theory," *Simply Psychology*, March 8, 2023, www.simplypsychology.org/bowlby.html.

30   Prarthana Franklin-Luther and Anthony A. Volk, "Social, Psychological, and Evolutionary Perspectives on Adoption," in *Oxford Bibliographies in Psychology,* ed. Dana S. Dunn (New York: Oxford, 2018), 1–12.

31   Diana Divecha, "Why Attachment Parenting Is Not the Same as Secure Attachment," *Greater Good Magazine,* May 2, 2018, greatergood.berkeley.edu/article/item/why_attachment_parenting_is_not_the_same_as_secure_attachment.

32   Jeffrey Kluger, "The Science Behind Dr. Sears: Does It Stand Up?" *Time*, May 10, 2012, ideas.time.com/2012/05/10/the-science-behind-dr-sears-does-it-stand-up/.

33   Pickert, "Man Who Remade Motherhood."

34   Kluger, "Science Behind Dr. Sears."

35   Divecha, "Why Attachment Parenting Is Not the Same."

36   Nathan A. Winner and Bonnie C. Nicholson, "Overparenting and Narcissism in Young Adults: The Mediating Role of Psychological Control," *Journal of Child and Family Studies* 27, no. 11 (July 2018): 3650–57.

37   Winter, "Harsh Realm of 'Gentle Parenting.'"

Chapter 2

38   Kate Julian, "What Happened to American Childhood?" *Atlantic,* May 2020, www.theatlantic.com/magazine/archive/2020/05/childhood-in-an-anxious-age/609079/.

39   Chris Segrin et al., "Parent and Child Traits Associated with Overparenting," *Journal of Social and Clinical Psychology* 32, no. 6 (May 2013): 569–95.

40   Madeline Levine, *The Price of Privilege: How Parental Pressure and Material Advantage Are Creating a Generation of Disconnected and Unhappy Kids* (New York: Harper Collins, 2006).

41   Jennifer Breheny Wallace, "Students in High-Achieving Schools Are Now Named an At-Risk Group, Study Says," *Washington Post*, September 26, 2019, www .washingtonpost.com/lifestyle/2019/09/26/ students-high-achieving-schools-are-now-named-an-at-risk-group/.

42   Hara Marano, *A Nation of Wimps: The High Cost of Invasive Parenting* (New York: Broadway Books, 2008).

43   Anna Brown, "Public and Private College Grads Rank About Equally in Life Satisfaction," Pew Research Center, May 19, 2014, www.pewresearch.org/short-reads/2014/05/19/ public-and-private-college-grads-rank-about-equally-in-life-satisfaction/.

44   William Stixrud, "It's Time to Tell Your Kids It Doesn't Matter Where They Go to College," *Time*, March 22, 2018, time.com/5210848/prestigious-college-doesnt-matter/.

45   Alison Escalante, "Why High Achievement Cultures Can Kill a Love of Learning," *Forbes*, March 2, 2021, www.forbes.com/sites/alisonescalante/2021/03/02/ why-high-achievement-cultures-can-kill-a-love-of-learning/.

46   Levine, *Price of Privilege*.

47   Purvi Mody, "Stop Telling Teens to Find Their Passions," Insight Education, www.insight-education.net/stop-telling-teens-find-passions/.

48   David Epstein, *Range: Why Generalists Triumph in a Specialized World* (New York: Riverhead Books, 2019).

Chapter 3

49   Elaine N. Aron, *The Highly Sensitive Child: Helping Our Children Thrive When the World Overwhelms Them* (New York: Harmony, 2002).

50   Jean-François Gariépy et al., "Social Learning in Humans and Other Animals," *Frontiers in Neuroscience* 8, no. 27 (March 2014): 58.

Chapter 4

51   Diana Divecha, "Family Conflict Is Normal; It's the Repair That Matters," *Greater Good Magazine*, October 27, 2020, greatergood.berkeley.edu/article/item/ family_conflict_is_normal_its_the_repair_that_matters.

52   Kenneth H. Rubin et al., "Peer Relationships," in *Developmental Science: An Advanced Textbook*, ed. Marc Bornstein and Michael Lamb (New York: Psychology Press, 2015), 587–644; Corinna Jenkins Tucker and David Finkelhor, "The State of Interventions for Sibling Conflict and Aggression: A Systematic Review," *Trauma, Violence, and Abuse* 18, no. 4 (December 2015): 396–406.

53   Karena Leo et al., "Conflict Management and Problem Solving as Relationship Maintenance," in *Relationship Maintenance: Theory, Process, and Context*, ed. Brian G. Ogolsky and J. Kale Monk (New York: Cambridge University Press, 2019), 194–214.

54   Lori D. Harach and Leon Kuczynski, "Construction and Maintenance of Parent–Child Relationships: Bidirectional Contributions from the Perspective of Parents," *Infant and Child Development* 14, no. 4 (November 2005): 327–43.

Chapter 5

55   "Clean Air Act Title IV Overview: Noise Pollution," United States Environmental Protection Agency, accessed September 26, 2022, www.epa.gov/clean-air-act-overview/clean-air-act-title-iv-noise-pollution.

56   S. W. Porges, "Orienting in a Defensive World: Mammalian Modifications of Our Evolutionary Heritage. A Polyvagal Theory," *Psychophysiology* 32, no. 4 (July 1995): 301–18.

57   Walter J. Freeman, "How and Why Brains Create Meaning from Sensory Information," *International Journal of Bifurcation and Chaos* 14, no. 2 (2004): 515–30.

58   Caitlyn Collett, "NTI Seminar: Neuroscientist Moran Cerf on How the Brain Processes Risk," *Atomic Pulse*, December 21, 2018, www.nti.org/atomic-pulse/nti-seminar-neuroscientist-moran-cerf-how-brain-processes-risk/; Moran Cerf, "Can You Trust Your Own Brain?" filmed March 13, 2020, in Porto, Portugal, TEDx video, 16:12, www.youtube.com/watch?v=1QAyn5e15LY.

59   Moran Cerf, email to author, June 18, 2019.

60   Andrea R. Beyer et al., "Risk Attitudes and Personality Traits Predict Perceptions of Benefits and Risks for Medicinal Products: A Field Study of European Medical Assessors," *Value in Health* 18, no. 1 (January 2015): 91–99.

61   Mark Williams and Danny Penman, *Mindfulness: An Eight-Week Plan for Finding Peace in a Frantic World* (New York: Rodale, 2011), 5.

62   Nigela Ahemaitijiang et al., "A Review of Mindful Parenting: Theory, Measurement, Correlates, and Outcomes," *Journal of Pacific Rim Psychology* 15 (December 2021): 1–20.

63   Alison Escalante, "New Research Finds Most People Are Not Using Mindfulness Correctly," *Forbes*, December 21, 2021, www.forbes.com/sites/alisonescalante/2021/12/21/new-research-finds-most-people-are-not-using-mindfulness-correctly/; Ellen Choi et al., "What Do People Mean When They Talk about Mindfulness?" *Clinical Psychology Review* 89, no. 2 (November 2021).

64   Jake Eagle and Michael Amster, *The Power of Awe: Overcome Burnout and Anxiety, Ease Chronic Pain, Find Clarity and Purpose—in Less Than 1 Minute per Day* (New York: Hachette Books, 2023), xiv.

65   "Jing Zuo," Wikipedia, updated August 27, 2022, https://en.wikipedia.org/wiki/Jing_zuo.

66   Antonia Blumberg, "Daily Meditation: To the Spirits," *HuffPost*, April 1, 2015, www.huffpost.com/entry/daily-meditation_n_6984400.

67   Terence Meyerhoefer et al., "Mindfulness Has Parallels to Indigenous Cultural Practices," *Psychiatric News*, October 26, 2022, psychnews.psychiatryonline.org/doi/10.1176/appi.pn.2022.11.11.28.

68   Victoria Dawson, "All Our Relations: Four Indigenous Lessons on Mindfulness," *Mindful*, November 7, 2021, www.mindful.org/all-our-relations-four-indigenous-lessons-on-mindfulness/.

69   Thomas L. Saltsman et al., "Facing the Facets: No Association Between Dispositional Mindfulness Facets and Positive Momentary Stress Responses During Active Stressors," *Personality and Social Psychology Bulletin* 47, no. 7 (July 2021): 1057–70.

70   Ying Chen, Laura D. Kubzansky, and Tyler J. VanderWeele, "Parental Warmth and Flourishing in Mid-life," *Social Science & Medicine* 220 (January 2019): 65–72; Alison Escalante, "Parents' Love Goes a Long Way," *Psychology Today*, February 26, 2019, www.psychologytoday.com/us/blog/shouldstorm/201902/parents-love-goes-long-way.

71   Ying Chen et al., "Positive Parenting Improves Multiple Aspects of Health and Well-Being in Young Adulthood," *Nature Human Behavior* 3, no. 7 (July 2019): 684–91; Alison Escalante, "In Parenting, Love Wins," *Psychology Today*, May 7, 2019, www.psychologytoday.com/us/blog/shouldstorm/201905/in-parenting-love-wins.

72   Ying Chen et al., "Positive Parenting."

73   Marcus Buckingham and Donald O. Clifton, *Now, Discover Your Strengths* (New York: The Free Press, 2001).

74   Mary Reckmeyer, *Strengths Based Parenting: Developing Your Children's Innate Talents* (Gallup Press, New York, 2016), 5.

75   Reckmeyer, *Strengths Based Parenting*, 245–47.

76   Reckmeyer, 269–71.

77   Reckmeyer, 30.

78   Reckmeyer, 21–23.

79   Reckmeyer, 38.

Chapter 6

80   Abigail A. Brown et al., "Examining the Energy Envelope and Associated Symptom Patterns in ME/CFS: Does Coping Matter?" *Chronic Illness* 9, no. 4 (December 2013): 302–11.

81   Frank Anderson, interview with author, August 4, 2022.

82   Dacher Keltner and Jonathan Haidt, "Approaching Awe, a Moral, Spiritual, and Aesthetic Emotion," *Cognition and Emotion* 17, no. 2 (March 2003): 297–314.

83   Michael Amster and Jake Eagle, "Stuck at Home? How to Find Awe and Beauty Indoors," *Greater Good*, April 15, 2020, greatergood.berkeley.edu/article/item/stuck_at_home_how_to_find_awe_beauty_indoors.

84   Alison Escalante, "Awe: The Instantaneous Way to Feel Good and Relieve Stress," *Psychology Today*, January 15, 2021, www.psychologytoday.com/intl/blog/shouldstorm/202101/awe-the-instantaneous-way-feel-good-and-relieve-stress.

85   Andrew Solomon, *Far from the Tree* (New York: Scribner, 2012), 5.

Chapter 7

86   Alison Escalante, "Voices in Your Head," *Psychology Today*, June 16, 2019, www.psychologytoday.com/intl/blog/shouldstorm/201906/the-voices-in-your-head.

87   Escalante, "The Voices in Your Head."

88   Frank Anderson, *Transcending Trauma: Healing Complex PTSD with Internal Family Systems Therapy* (Eau Claire, WI: PESI Publishing, 2021).

89   Anderson, interview.

90   Anderson, interview.

91   Alison Escalante, "Do You Ever Wonder What's Going on Inside Your Child's Head?" *Psychology Today*, July 3, 2019, www.psychologytoday.com/us/blog/shouldstorm/201907/do-you-ever-wonder-whats-going-in-your-childs-head.

92   Escalante, "Do You Ever Wonder."

93   Escalante, "Do You Ever Wonder."

94   Deb Dana, interview with author, March 18, 2019.

95   Tina Payne Bryson, interview with author, January 6, 2023.

96   Bryson, interview.

97   Bryson, interview.

98   Bryson, interview.

99   Bryson, interview.

100   Bryson, interview.

101   Winter, "Harsh Realm of 'Gentle Parenting.'"

102   Bryson, interview.

103   Jenny S. Radesky et al., "Longitudinal Associations Between Use of Mobile Devices for Calming and Emotional Reactivity and Executive Functioning in Children Aged 3 to 5 Years," *JAMA Pediatrics* 177, no. 1 (January 2023): 62–70.

Chapter 8

104   Barton Goldsmith, "10 Tips for Holding a Family Meeting," *Psychology Today*, September 5, 2012, www.psychologytoday.com/intl/blog/emotional-fitness/201209/10-tips-holding-family-meeting.

105   Te-Ping Chen, "What CEOs Are Getting Wrong about the Future of Work—and How to Make It Right," *Wall Street Journal*, February 17, 2023, www.wsj.com/articles/what-ceos-are-getting- wrong-about-the-future-of-workand-how-to-make-it-right-8a84e279.

106   Chen, "What CEOs Are Getting Wrong."

107 Po Bronson and Ashley Merryman, *NurtureShock: New Thinking about Children* (New York: Hachette Book Group, 2009), 15.

108 Imed Bouchrika, "How Not to Talk to Your Child: Raising Confident, Well-Adjusted Kids," *Research.com*, September 26, 2022, research.com/education/how-not-to-talk-to-your-child.

109 Li Zhao et al., "Praising Young Children for Being Smart Promotes Cheating," *Psychological Science* 28, no. 12 (December 2017): 1868–70.

110 Ross Greene, interview with author, January 4, 2023.

111 University of Gothenburg, "Young Children Are Skilled Negotiators, Swedish Research Finds," *ScienceDaily*, June 24, 2010, www.sciencedaily.com/releases/2010/06/100621101206.htm.

112 Molly Kern and Terri R. Kurtzberg, "How to Negotiate…with Your Kids," *Harvard Business Review,* May 29, 2020, hbr.org/2020/05/how-to-negotiate-with-your-kids.

113 PON staff, "Ask A Negotiation Expert: The Surprising Benefits of Negotiating with Your Kids," Program on Negotiation, Harvard Law School, December 1, 2020, www.pon.harvard.edu/daily/negotiation-skills-daily/ask-a-negotiation-expert-the-surprising-benefits-of-negotiating-with-your-kids-nb/.

114 Greene, interview.

115 Greene, interview.

116 Eli Lebowitz and Yaara Shimshoni, "The SPACE Program: How Parents Can Help Children Overcome Anxiety," Anxiety and Depression Association of America, June 8, 2020, adaa.org/webinar/professional/space-program-how-parents-can-help-children-overcome-anxiety; Eli R. Lebowitz, *Breaking Free of Child Anxiety and OCD: A Scientifically Proven Program for Parents* (New York: Oxford University Press, 2021).

117 Families in the United States may be able to access developmental therapies through government-sponsored insurance plans, therapy centers that offer financially sensitive sliding scales, and public schools and preschools that offer services during the school day. If scheduling around work is a challenge, talk to your human resources department about taking protected time for appointments under the US Family and Medical Leave Act (FMLA).

118 Lebowitz and Shimshoni, "SPACE Program"; Lebowitz, *Breaking Free.*

Chapter 9

119 Joe L. Frost, *A History of Children's Play and Play Environments* (New York: Routledge, 2009).

120 "UN Convention on the Rights of the Child," International Play Association, accessed February 26, 2023, ipaworld.org/childs-right-to-play/uncrc-article-31/un-convention-on-the-rights-of-the-child-1/.

121 Kenneth R. Ginsburg, the Committee on Communications, and the Committee on Psychosocial Aspects of Child and Family Health, "The Importance of Play in Promoting Healthy Child Development and Maintaining Strong Parent-Child Bonds," *Pediatrics* 119, no. 1 (January 2007): 182–91.

122 Sofia Quaglia, "Do Bees Play? A Groundbreaking Study Says Yes," *National Geographic,* October 27, 2022, www.nationalgeographic.com/animals/article/bees-can-play-study-shows-bumblebees-insect-intelligence.

123 Stuart Brown, *Play: How It Shapes the Brain, Opens the Imagination, and Invigorates the Soul* (New York: Avery, 2010).

124 Yung-Wei Lin and Sue C. Bratton, "A Meta-Analytic Review of Child-Centered Play Therapy Approaches," *Journal of Counseling & Development* 93, no. 1 (January 2015): 45–58; Dee C. Ray, "Impact of Play Therapy on Parent-Child Relationship Stress at a Mental Health Training Setting," *British Journal of Guidance & Counselling* 36, no. 2 (2008): 165–87; Kate Wilson and Virginia Ryan, "Helping Parents by Working with Their Children in Individual Child Therapy," *Child & Family Social Work* 6, no. 3 (August 2001): 209–17.

125 Donna B. Pincus, *Growing Up Brave: Expert Strategies for Helping Your Child Overcome Fear, Stress, and Anxiety* (New York: Little, Brown and Company, 2012), 74.

126 Pincus, *Growing Up Brave,* 74.

127 Pincus, 75–76.

128 Pincus, 76–81.

129 Diana D. Coyl-Shepherd and Colleen Hanlon, "Family Play and Leisure Activities: Correlates of Parents' and Children's Socio-emotional Well-Being," *International Journal of Play* 2, no. 3 (2013): 254–72.

130 S. E. Duff, "A Study of the Effects of Group Family Play on Family Relations," *International Journal of Play Therapy* 5, no. 2 (1996): 81–93.

131 Ginsburg, the Committee on Communications, and the Committee on Psychosocial Aspects of Child and Family Health, "Importance of Play."

132 Ginsburg, the Committee on Communications, and the Committee on Psychosocial Aspects of Child and Family Health, "Importance of Play."

133 University of Gothenburg, "Young Children Are Skilled Negotiators."

134 Mia Heikkilä et al., "Barns deltagande i förskole-och daghemskontext under inledningen av coronavirusets utbrott i Finland och Sverige," *BARN* 38, no. 2 (2020).

135 Mariana Brussoni et al., "Risky Play and Children's Safety: Balancing Priorities for Optimal Child Development," *International Journal of Environmental Research and Public Health* 9, no. 9 (2012): 3134–48.

INDEX

Index

Index